FINDING THE ENERGY

Rick Schroder

Durban House

Printed in the United States of America.

For information address:

Durban House Press, Inc.
5001 LBJ Freeway, Suite 700
Dallas, Texas 75244

Library of Congress Cataloging-in-Publication Data

Schroder, Rick

Finding the Energy/Rick Schroder

Library of Congress Control Number: 2007943816

p. cm.

ISBN: 987-0-9800067-5-9
0-9800067-5-9

First Edition

10 9 8 7 6 5 4 3 2 1

Visit our Web site at
http://www.durbanhouse.com

In Memory of

Richard Wiederholt

Because of you my life has changed in ways I could not have imagined when we first met. I still draw upon you for inspiration and occasionally, courage.

Acknowledgements

Journaling was something I picked up in high school and have continued in some fashion for most of my life. Still, as much as I enjoy spending quiet time capturing my thoughts, a book was not something I thought was on the horizon. It really wasn't until I met Richard Wiederholt that the idea began to take root. Richard was a great coach and friend. After writing my coming out story, I shared some of my journal with him. It was at that point that he suggested I consider a book. I will always be grateful to him for his nurturing and encouragement. This book is a testament to his ability to see the potential in people.

As with any book, there were several versions of the draft manuscript. In order to really bring the book to life, I relied on Mark Chesler for his insights on the overall manuscript's direction and flow. My thanks to Donna Zimmer for suggesting I bring more of myself to the book, and the use of the condo in Florida to work on revisions. Tomas Leal provided some great suggestions on the overall organization and structure of the manuscript. Liz Winfeld, Stephen Young, Bill Proudman and Michael Welp offered some great advice to a struggling new writer and really helped me maneuver the publishing world. My special thanks to David Fortsch for his early interest in my development as a student and the review of my manuscript. Bob Middlemiss is truly a fine editor, and I look forward to working with him again on other projects.

I cannot fully express my gratitude to Judith Moorad and Steve Miller for their support, leadership, guidance, and advice throughout my career. I was very fortunate to have the opportunity to learn and grow under their wings.

Table of Contents

Preface

While a number of books address coming out in the workplace and the issues facing gay, lesbian, bisexual, and transgender (GLBT) people, I have not encountered any that really explored the journey, life and experiences that followed for someone in the workplace. In October 1994 I made a conscious decision to come out at work in the conservative oil and gas industry. As a result my life took a series of notable turns, leading to new horizons, opening doors to opportunities, and presenting formidable challenges.

Throughout the book I refer to various terms which may not be familiar to all readers. Some of these terms are "coming out," "the closet," "sexual orientation," "gender identity," and "transgender." I do not intend to go into an exhaustive review, but just to provide basic definitions to create a context for these terms in the overall discussion.

The expression "coming out" refers to a person's no longer hiding his or her sexual identity from others. The individual makes a profoundly personal decision to stop hiding the reality that he or she is gay, lesbian, bisexual or transgender. The other side of the coin is life in the "closet," a term used to describe the hiding or suppression of an individual's sexual orientation. Many GLBT people live life in the closet, expending enormous effort to keep their personal lives hidden from the rest of the world.

Accepted social norms provide for heterosexuals to display their sexual identity on a regular basis: the wedding band on a finger, pictures of a spouse and/or children in the office, talking about family activities over the weekend, etc. Just as being heterosexual is a journey through life, so is being lesbian, gay, bisexual or transgender. The decision of how and when to come out is different for each individual.

"Sexual orientation" is a term used to describe the physical attraction an individual may have toward another. Being heterosexual and homosexual are both examples of sexual orientation. This is not something unique to the GLBT community. Again, cultural norms prescribe that males are masculine in their gender expression and females are feminine. In reality, how a person expresses his or her gender is not necessarily an indication of sexual orientation. For example, a male demonstrating some feminine characteristics in body language or gestures may be considered "straight" or heterosexual. Straight is a commonly used term synonymous with heterosexual behavior.

Gender identity tackles the psychological gender role of a person, which may or may not be aligned with the gender assigned at birth. Gender dysphoria is the condition in which gender organs are not aligned with a person's gender identity. People who suffer from gender dysphoria, a diagnosis recognized by the American Psychiatric Association, may decide to seek medical treatment to reconcile the dichotomy between gender identity and sex at birth. Undergoing treatment is in itself a journey, requiring years of counseling, hormone treatments, and possibly surgeries.

In the context of this book I use the term "transgender" as an umbrella for the broader community that includes cross-dressers, transsexuals, transvestites and others when referring to the "T" in GLBT. I also use the term in reference to specific individuals in the book who are working through their gender dysphoria.

To really understand the reasons for my coming out, I have to explore finding myself. The 1970s and 1980s provided the backdrop, a time of rising visibility for the GLBT community, some good experiences and some not so good. I was all too familiar with the stigma rural America attached to the term "gay." It was a stereotype that often included words like *faggot*, *queer*, *diseased*, *pedophile*, *feminine*, and *dirty*. In the '70s a subculture emerged, and the '80s saw the rise of a virus that seemed at the time to specifically target gay men in the community—HIV/AIDS.

The first couple of chapters of this book explore my upbringing, life as it evolved after my leaving for college, then my transitioning from academia into the work environment, and my decision-making process for one day coming out at work. For much of this time I lived in small towns and cities, finally reaching Los Angeles in the late 1980s. While I had explored my sexual orientation in the early '80s, I really hadn't acted on it until the mid 1980s. The AIDS epidemic was in full swing and influenced my decisions about dating. The last thing I wanted was to get sick with what at the time was a terminal illness.

It really wasn't until the 1990s that I began to confront my fears about HIV/AIDS. After moving to Houston, Texas, I made friends with several people who were HIV-positive. Most have died, including a mentor and dear friend who showed me that fears are best conquered by knowledge and learning.

The journey subsequent to coming out follows my life from a successful technical career through a transition leading to assignments in the heart of a corporation where I had a chance to engage and influence senior leaders and work directly with a CEO on GLBT workplace policies. Along the road, I influenced adding sexual orientation to the non-discrimination policy, partnered with others to create a GLBT employee network, pursued obtaining domestic partnership benefits, engaged senior leaders in their learning about GLBT workplace issues, learned about transgender issues and became an ally, and promoted company support for GLBT policies at the local, state and federal level.

True to my nature of being a pack rat, I kept notes and journals along the way to help relive some of the earlier years. I found myself reflecting on episodes of my life and revisiting some of the behaviors of others and the feelings I experienced at the time. It's very difficult for me to share what I'm feeling. My tendency is to move away from emotional behavior and talk instead to the rational response. This engagement of the mind and suppression of the heart was a behavior I felt was necessary for me to show strength.

Both the heart and mind ultimately play into the crafting of a response or modeling of an expected behavior. For this reason I will consciously attempt to describe my feelings at the time and how they influenced my behavior. Ultimately I think it's important to understand how both are impacted by the actions of others and how we react in response.

When I came out at work, I had no intention of changing the workplace or a company, just a desire to live my own life. Over time circumstances shifted, and I found myself pursuing the creation of a safe, open workplace where everyone is treated with dignity and respect and has the ability to achieve his or her potential. My hope is that readers will garner some value from this book to apply in their own endeavors or journeys in the workplace.

1 Growing Up to Find My Closet

One sunny fall day in 1994, a guy went to work like any other day. There was nothing on his "To Do" list about changing a company, or his life, for that matter. He just wanted to finish his assignment for the refinery in Louisiana and go home. Nothing was unusual about that day, until he checked e-mails in the afternoon before running off to the airport to fly home. He saw a note from his boss announcing that a co-worker was leaving the company. The e-mail would have been a non-event had it not been for one thing—the colleague's reason for leaving. He was HIV-positive and had a declining T-cell count.

At that moment the employee blinked, reading the note again to make sure he wasn't imagining things. The note was real, and he had two options: press the delete button, or reply to his boss requesting more information. After hesitating for what seemed an eternity, he chose the latter.

The words in the note had caused something inside him to snap. For selfish motives, he was angry that the co-worker was leaving. He was certain the co-worker was gay, even though nothing about sexual orientation was mentioned in the note. He couldn't believe his colleague was walking out the door—he had to talk to him. The employee was sure his co-worker could relate to what he was feeling at that point in his career about life in the workplace. If only they could talk.

What followed were life changing events, unforeseen challenges, and another path. It was as if a door suddenly appeared and offered a tempting curiosity of what might be on the other side. By replying to the e-mail, the employee opened the door, peering into a different place, a different path through life yet unexplored.

About a month after replying to the e-mail, a series of events culminated with the employee's "coming out" at work. Coming out is a reconciliation of self in a heterosexual world where homosexuality is not the socially constructed norm. With coaching and guidance from mentors and leaders, he strove to educate a company on gay, lesbian, bisexual and transgender (GLBT) issues in the workplace.

Eventually those conversations were influential in adding sexual orientation to the company non-discrimination policy. With the change to the non-discrimination policy, the employee published his coming out story in the Houston GLBT monthly, *Out Smart* magazine. When the magazine issue hit the streets, phone calls and e-mails started pouring into his office from others in the company he had never met. They had all seen the story and thought it was great.

One person was so moved by the article that he too decided to come out in the workplace. They teamed up and began the creation of Shell's GLBT employee network group. That led to instituting domestic partner benefits, developing strategies for education and awareness, engaging leaders in the company on workplace issues, and building Shell's outreach to the GLBT community. Contributions from the Shell Oil Company Foundation were made to GLBT charities, and eventually the company endorsed the Employment Non-Discrimination Act (ENDA). So much tangible progress over a relatively short period of time from a company long viewed as a bastion carrying the banner for an industry known for its conservatism. Bastions are built by people, and for better or worse, they change with the people that lead them.

So whatever happened to that guy who in 1994 decided to hit the reply button? I decided to capture my experiences and share what I have learned, thinking it might be of value to others striving to create safe, open workplaces where people are treated with dignity and respect, and have the opportunity to achieve their full potential.

Much of what transpired was directly tied to reconciling my sexual orientation with society's expectations. For as long as I can remember I've been attracted to guys. One of my earliest recollections is when I was a young boy about eight years old, watching an episode of the original *Star Trek* series. In the episode a shirtless Sulu was running around the *Enterprise* with a fencing foil. I found myself riveted to Sulu. I didn't know why, only that I had a deep sense or internal desire to be close to him.

The societal values imprinted upon me while growing up on a family-owned dairy in Smyrna, a conservative upstate New York hamlet, suggested my desires to be close to another man were not to be condoned. My family's references to homosexuals as "homos," "queers," and "fags" reinforced the unacceptability of such behavior during my upbringing. True to cultural norms, any behaviors not representative of a normal, healthy, masculine boy were frowned upon or squelched.

No one in my family was gay—or at least, no one was letting on. While I felt affection for other males, I was confused about why grownups found the issue so uncomfortable. I struggled with why society vilified feeling a sense of affection or comfort with someone else of the same sex.

My feelings were something I wasn't about to discuss with anyone—the social norm was that guys don't have feelings. Yet actions can speak louder than words, and reflecting on my youth, there were a number of instances of self-betrayal.

The farms were far enough apart that I had few friends my age. Most of my social interactions began at age four, when I entered school. Smyrna still had a grade school then—there were about fifteen students in my class. Each class had one teacher that taught all the subjects. During recess most children went outside to play, some may have been held inside to catch up on work, and a few others might take up an activity hosted by one of the teachers. The fifth grade teacher, for example, hosted a knitting circle during the recess hour for any girls interested in learning the craft.

Not one to be inhibited, I asked if I too could learn to knit. An astonished teacher saw no harm, and I joined the girls during recess. When I asked my mother for some yarn and needles, my father raised a weary eyebrow. My mother thought it was cute, but my father worried about how I would be perceived by the other boys in school. Reluctantly he went along with it, hoping my interest was just a "phase" that would pass. Eventually I did lose interest, but not before learning how to do cable stitches and make a scarf.

High school presented other difficulties. With the onset of puberty there were things about my body I didn't completely understand. Rather than help me through this awkward phase of life, my parents left it up to me to figure out. So I did what any budding teenager would do—I talked to my friends. The message was pretty consistent—you're a guy, you need to chase women. I was a guy who preferred home economics classes to industrial arts, and I was supposed to chase women?

As a freshman, I became well aware of how rigorously societal norms could be enforced. A friend and I were walking through the commons one day on our way to lunch. Ahead of us were a group of boys beating up my friend's younger brother. The younger brother had very feminine characteristics, and my friend had relayed that he liked dressing in girl's clothes. I asked if he was going to help his brother—his response was that the younger brother got what he deserved. As much as I disagreed, I didn't go to his brother's defense either. My disagreement had more to do with the physical violence than the reason that prompted the beating. The younger brother was being punished by his peers for acting on his feelings and not conforming to society's definition of "normal."

A few years ago, while reading my hometown newspaper, I saw an obituary for my friend's mom. The write-up stated that the younger brother had predeceased her. He died in his early twenties, shortly after high school. As I reflect on the situation, I realize he was transgender. I didn't know what to make of him at the time. It wasn't like I could go to the library and ask for a book explaining his condition, or that my teachers in health class or biology were going to give everyone a lecture on sexual orientation or gender identity. Only decades later did I realize he was brought into this world and rejected simply because he didn't fit into an acceptable social mold.

One of my most horrifying experiences was gym class. The showers were one big bullpen with nozzles along all the walls. I was never sure how I would react to seeing other naked classmates. Not wanting to risk personal embarrassment and being labeled a "fag," I tried to be one of the last people in the showers. I walked in with my eyes straight ahead, looking for a corner shower so I could keep my back to others. I also made an effort to pick a locker that wasn't in one of the main rows with everyone else's.

Growing up on a family-operated dairy made dating tough. I sensed some concern from my parents through their inquiries about whether I was interested in anyone. My older brother had been dating for a while. Even my younger sister was starting to see some boys. Fortunately, I found a girlfriend during my last two years of high school, and my parents seemed to breathe a sigh of relief.

Of course, no one ever believed she and I were staying up until the wee hours of the morning baking cookies and drinking sangria. While I loved her very much, I wasn't physically interested in doing anything other than kissing and cuddling. She wanted to wait until marriage to have sex, and that suited me just fine.

During my first year of college, she dumped me for someone else. Devastated by the experience, I buried myself in school and farm work. I was attending a junior college near home, commuting to classes every day and doing my farm chores in the early morning and evening.

I wasn't the only one having relationship problems—this was a time in my life when the normal family structure and "Rockwellian" values disintegrated before my eyes. The family was strained irreparably to the point of breaking, my parents entering into a protracted and vicious divorce. I was ostracized by both of them for my reluctance to side with one over the other. On the farm I took refuge with my grandmother, who saw the divorce as a senseless, agonizing waste of time—sharp lady. With all the fighting, my grandmother was all the family I had left.

I looked forward to classes my first two years of college. School was a refuge from home. Feeling very much alone for the first time in my life, I longed for companionship. After being dropped by my high school sweetheart, I really needed to fill a void, but was frustrated about how. I was really struggling with my affection for men. While I had women friends, I found myself more interested in hanging out with guys.

After junior college I decided to go away for school, far away. I picked Idaho—the school had a great geology program and was far from my troubled home environment in upstate New York—the things I wanted most. With my family situation in turmoil, I realized I could never turn to them in a time of need and had to be prepared to fend for myself in life. My grandmother helped me when she could, using her matriarchal influence to ensure I would at least get a good education. So I knuckled under and concentrated on my studies.

During my undergraduate years there was no shortage of attractive women, but I wasn't asking them out. No matter how hard I fought the impulse, deep inside I wanted to be with a man. The pressures of acting "normal," the anxiety over being discovered, and the desire to be emotionally and physically close to someone I loved were so contradicting they were often more than I could bear. I often wonder how I lived through those times, and realize why many do not.

After receiving my bachelor's degree, I went home for the summer before heading off to graduate school in the fall. Neither of my parents attended my graduation. My father met me at the airport, very happy I was home. Before going to the farm he wanted to stop by my mother's residence. I had heard that after four years of fighting, they had finally reached a settlement. I thought it honorable a father would set aside his differences, wanting his son to see his mother. I should have realized there might be another motive.

When we arrived at my mom's apartment, the motive became clear—I was the only person my parents could agree on to witness their divorce papers. This was my reward for being a loving son to both who would side with neither during their fighting. I knew graduate school would not afford the luxury of many trips home, and once again I was looking forward to school.

While I was a graduate student in the early '80s, the reality of being gay finally permeated the thick blanket of denial I'd wrapped myself in since my youth. The final straw occurred when a student approached me on a warm spring afternoon in 1985 as I was leaving class. We struck up a conversation on the sidewalk that ended moments later with him agreeing to come over to my place that evening to study.

What was I thinking? I'd just invited someone over to my place that I had never met before. All I knew about him was his name, yet deep inside I knew this was okay. In fact, I was actually feeling excited about having him over.

He arrived at the appointed time. His subject was history, and I was working through some material on crystallography—we both ended up studying anatomy instead. Being with him felt so comfortable and natural. I wanted him to stay with me that night, but as hard as I tried, he wouldn't.

As he walked out the door, I began analyzing in my mind what had just happened—panic, anxiety and paranoia engulfed my thoughts. Someone must have been setting me up for a fall.

What other reason could he have had for picking me out on the sidewalk? Why else would he have to leave and not stay the night? What better way to take out a popular graduate student then exposing him as a homosexual? I was uncontrollably shaking and had to get out of the house.

All the worst-case scenarios of what would happen if people found out I had had sex with another male were swirling in my head. I couldn't be discovered. My career would be destroyed before it began. I felt helpless—everything was going up in flames and was out of my control. I was literally driving myself crazy.

To calm my nerves I had to get my mind on something else. I ran back to campus that night to the geology department, a popular place for undergraduates struggling with their lab work, hoping a graduate student would show up and help them out. I was in luck—there were several students in one of the labs. Immersing myself in their problems, the anxiety and panic slowly faded as the rational, technical side of my brain took over.

More than anything, I was afraid of failing. I was trying to finish a master's degree and running desperately short of money. My stipends from the university were running out that summer. My father was reluctant to co-sign any more student loans. The experience with the guy coming over to study had put me very close to the emotional brink.

The stress and confusion associated with who and what I was at a very important juncture in life was considerable. One thing was apparent—to be successful, I needed to organize my priorities. Of all the thoughts on my mind, two seemed irreconcilable—a career and my sexual orientation. Intuitively, I sensed that the world wouldn't afford many opportunities to an openly gay geologist.

So at the age of 25, knowing very little about gay life, or myself, I naively decided to enter the safety of the closet. "The closet" is a term often used by members of the GLBT community to describe the isolation of hiding their sexual orientation from the rest of the world. For me the closet would be what I went home to—another life. It provided "space" where I could be myself, a safe harbor from the surrounding world. Basically, my social and professional lives couldn't become intertwined. All of my personal and social involvement would be in the closet, kept a safe distance from straight friends, family, and the workplace.

In reflection, the toughest challenge was keeping the "door" locked. I did many things over the years to protect my closet—lying about my personal life, misleading others by creating shams, creating fictional friends and family. I learned all the tricks of the trade. Rather than become victim to the "rumor mill," I learned to manipulate it as a vehicle for maintaining my heterosexual identity.

Ultimately, I created a paradox where no one, including myself, would really know me. After a while of fabricating stories and friends I actually began to forget who and what I was, and the values I believed in. There was a huge commitment of time and effort to keep the stories straight—the slightest slip might raise eyebrows, lead others to not trust me, or expose my secret and label me a liar and a charlatan.

With no clear rationale in mind, I also created a self-imposed time limit of ten years on my life in the closet. The incubation time was supposed to make me stronger, more certain of who or what I was. The justification for the closet was all about perception; work hard and become a good role model for the GLBT community. The underlying premise: when the day came and society wanted to pass judgment, they'd have to think pretty damn hard before condemning me on the basis of prejudice.

Making this work meant more than being the best professionally; it also meant being socially responsible and achieving financial stability. Treating people with respect, helping others in need, not passing judgment, so much stuff! I wasn't sure the aspirations were realistic, let alone achievable.

With something of a plan in place, I left college in the fall of 1985. With a partially completed thesis in tow, I began life in a corporate closet. Rockwell International had hired me on a project at the Hanford site located in southeast Washington State. I was both excited and apprehensive about the job. The assignment required a Department of Energy clearance, which meant completing an application that included inquiries about one's sexual orientation. By answering the questions, I locked the door on the closet.

The application was the first obvious institutional barrier that could have selectively eliminated me from a great paying job and a shot at beginning a successful career. It gnawed at the very marrow of my values, trust and honesty. If I responded honestly, the job could evaporate before my eyes. If I lied, it could be the start of my career and financial stability, something I needed desperately at the time. As it was, I had to borrow money from my advisor at school to be able to afford to move. Not having been "out" up to that point in my life meant nothing was going to show up when they did the security check.

With the checking of a box, my career began. I have yet to understand why being gay was more of a risk to security than being straight. After all, there are more heterosexuals in the world than gay people. I guess heterosexuals don't tend to engage in unseen sexual indiscretions that might be viewed as a risk to security —one only has to pick up a newspaper to find the fallacy in this statement.

Notably, over the years government thinking progressed and the question on the application referring to one's sexual orientation was eventually removed from the security petition. However, that hasn't stopped the current administration from revisiting the wording about how one's sexual orientation figures into a security clearance. Could it be *déjà vu*?

Looking back over the early years of my life, there are a number of observations that stand out for me:

- I was aware of my attraction to others of the same gender at an early age, before puberty, when social norms and behaviors were beginning to establish how I should self-identify in life.

- Although I wasn't talking about my interest in other males, some of my behaviors during my upbringing spoke for me as being questionable given society's expectations of a healthy, straight, masculine male.

- Feelings are not something to be shown or shared—as a male I was expected to be tough, rugged, and unemotional. To achieve this image I strove to be logical, studious and physically hard working.

- While my sexual orientation differed from socially constructed norms, I didn't understand why and had no resources, support groups or people I could trust to help me understand why I was different.

- Given society's deep-rooted prejudices toward the GLBT community, I chose to begin my career in the closet in order to establish myself professionally and become financially stable.

- My life became a huge paradox. I felt compelled to hide in the closet and manipulate situations and people to maintain the lie about my sexual orientation. Yet at the same time, I strove to build trust, treat people with respect, help those in need, and not judge others. I set the stage to live two lives.

2 The Struggles of a Career

The first few years in the closet proved difficult, requiring tremendous energy, discipline, patience and attention to managing life in two worlds. The three small cities of Richland, Kennewick and Pasco straddle the convergence of the Snake, Yakima and Columbia rivers. While the regional population was substantial, there was nothing in the way of a GLBT community, and meeting other gay people proved daunting.

I was settling in at work, making friends, progressing on my thesis, and doing the "straight scene" outside of work. For a while the thesis was a convenient excuse, a place of retreat when people asked about whom I was dating. When co-workers asked about my personal life, I'd tell them my graduate degree was my priority, which was partially true.

There were other challenges along the way. A few months into the job I became aware of a co-worker who was doing everything in her power to get me fired. I was being retaliated against, not because of my sexual orientation, but because I was perceived as a white heterosexual male rewarded more favorably by the system. Her motive: the inconsistencies in the hiring practices of the company, something I had absolutely no control over. The last thing I wanted or needed was additional attention. Fortunately, common sense intervened and management put us on separate projects.

Ironically, everything seems to boil down to how we're perceived by others. I left that job and company in 1987, but throughout my career I've periodically reflected on the situation. I viewed the experience for a long time as another reason for staying in the closet. After all, if I could be retaliated against for being a straight white male, what would happen if they discovered my real sexual orientation?

In spite of what was playing out at work and the societal obstacles and barriers to finding a GLBT community, I did manage to ferret out a guy with whom I became romantically involved. We met through a mutual friend who was unaware either of us was gay. Under the circumstances of how we met and where we were living, it took a couple of months for us to take the leap of coming out to each other, but we got there. We fell in love.

Up to that point in life I had never really had a boyfriend. I had met a couple of people and we had dated a bit, but none was interested in a relationship. Mike was different. We spent weeks getting to know each other. Our time together consisted of quiet walks along the Snake River with his Wheaton terrier or going to a movie. At one point we tried racquetball, but it just wasn't my sport. All the time we kept our relationship very quiet, a challenge given that one of my colleagues lived across the street from Mike and would inquire about my weekends at his house. When the questions came up, the story was the same—we were just friends.

After several months, with little explanation I was dumped and heartbroken. At work people could tell something was wrong, but I couldn't share my secret or look to them for support. The only person I could confide in was the one who had chosen to end our relationship. I found myself wanting to fill the void somehow, yet I was too emotionally unstable to pull my life back together.

Life became a series of mood swings, bouts with depression, and at times uncontrollable crying sessions. I couldn't go to my family, friends, or even Mike, for that matter. I suppressed as much pain as possible, looking for alternatives to bide the time in hopes the emotional wounds would heal. Again, I let the technical side of my brain take over, burying myself in my thesis, which I successfully defended in the spring of 1987.

Finishing the thesis made me restless—I had more free time on my hands and was dwelling on my failed relationship with Mike. It was time to get out of the small towns and into the big city. I needed more of a sense of who I was and more familiarity with my own community.

In late 1987 I took the plunge and moved to Los Angeles, taking a job with a small environmental company that offered a number of career opportunities. I was still very wary of being "out" in the workplace. I knew I'd have to prove myself all over again. Work and personal life would continue to remain separate, but at least now I could build a gay-friendly support network. I spent much of my weekends exploring West Hollywood, meeting people and dating. While I never completely got over Mike, the surroundings of West Hollywood and Los Angeles provided a potent anesthesia.

HIV/AIDS made the 1980s and beyond a scary time for the GLBT community. At the time there were still many unanswered questions about what caused the HIV infection or how it spread. In rural areas of the country I had been exposed to during the early years of the epidemic, little attention seemed to be paid to HIV/AIDS. In general, society seemed ambivalent to the epidemic until it took on the faces of celebrities and children, and groups like ACT UP brought visibility to the crisis.

My perception at the time was that once one was diagnosed HIV-positive, there was no more hiding, because so much of the media exposure about HIV/AIDS at the time focused on gay men. There would be no more plan and no control over how events would unfold—my career could be wrecked and I would become another statistic, largely ignored. The possibility of becoming infected scared me as I gingerly stepped into the L.A. dating scene.

At work I was assigned to the project team responsible for the Shell Oil contract. Eventually I progressed from a field assignment to project manager, and finally to team leader for the contract. With each move came more responsibility and more interface with the client.

I worked long and hard building a reputation of being credible and trustworthy in my profession. In the role of team leader I was continually balancing the needs of the client, the requirements of the agency, and the profitability of the consulting firm. Shell was a very sophisticated client, always challenging to my professional growth and development.

As a hydrogeologist, I admired Shell as a company. During my academic years in geology I had often read of their achievements and thought of working there one day. But the universities I had attended weren't on Shell's list of schools for recruiting. Working on the contract for Shell was as close to working for them as I ever thought I'd get.

After a couple of years in Los Angeles, my social life was emerging. While I had a number of straight friends who had followed me to L.A. for work, I also had the beginnings of a network of gay friends—none of whom were out at work. Sometimes our conversations would drift to our fears of being "outted" at work. When the topic came up I couldn't help but think about "the plan" I'd formulated in years past while at graduate school.

I was halfway through my self-imposed internment in the closet that I had arbitrarily established while in graduate school. As I dwelled on life so far, different scenarios came to mind about transitioning to a world outside the closet—it became very obvious that coming out was going to be more complicated than getting up one morning in 1995, going to work and saying, "I'm queer, I'm here, get used to it." It wasn't clear to me how others might react to the news. To gain some sense of how my sexual orientation might be received, I decided to test my secret with some of my straight friends.

I began telling some straight friends about my sexual orientation in the spring of 1990. Over the years I had worked hard to cultivate some wonderful relationships for a couple of reasons. First, my family hadn't been much of a family, causing me to rely more on friends as surrogates in times of need. Secondly, I knew one day I would have to explain my sexual orientation to all my straight friends, and I wanted them to think hard about what our relationship really meant to each of us.

The ordeal of building friendships had become complex, time-consuming, and arduous over the years. Paradigms, as well as my values and beliefs, were shifting. My sense of a "traditional" family had evaporated, while concepts pertaining to relationships and trust began to condense. Meeting someone and calling him "friend" was no longer good enough. I had to define what friendship meant to me—what it would look like over time, and how it would evolve.

I was establishing a complex sense of networking built on nurturing strong and meaningful relationships. Building trust was more than words, requiring tangible evidence and commitment to the relationships. The investments I've made over the years in these relationships have for better or worse taken their toll—the distillate being a series of strong, lasting friendships spanning more than 20 years.

Much to my pleasant surprise, none of my straight friends abandoned me as I came out to them. Some had suspected I was gay and were waiting for me to tell them—so much for self-perceptions of being straight. To this day they remain a foundation upon whom I rely for support and encouragement.

The work environment was very competitive, and a rumor of being gay, even at a business in L.A.., could scuttle a career. I was also finding it more difficult to hide my sexual orientation as I moved up in the company. People wanted to know more about my social life, who I was seeing and the events of the weekend. Attending company social functions was an unwritten expectation, and who was on your arm was duly noted.

Telling my friends at work that I was gay was going to be a little more challenging than telling my other friends had been. I'd been fortunate in having a few of my friends join me at the consulting firm. Among them was Mike (the man I'd loved and lost in Washington State)—he worked in the lab, a separate building just a block down the street. At that stage in our lives we were still reconciling differences, negotiating a different relationship, and trying to build a lasting friendship. With the exception of Mike, none of my colleagues or friends at the firm knew I was gay.

Another friend was the person who had originally introduced us—he was on my project team. By outing myself to the team, I had to be careful not to implicate Mike in the discussion or accidentally "out" him. Inevitably, questions about Mike did come up, and my response was short and terse—Mike and I were just friends. After all, what Mike and I had shared in the Tri-cities was between him and me.

As I had developed and cultivated each of these friendships one by one, I had also chosen to tell each of them individually about my sexual orientation. This approach created an opportunity for me to work through their individual questions and issues without other distractions. This was more manageable for me than being subjected to inquiries, issues and reactions from a group, which I felt would be too overwhelming to bear or control.

The process was straightforward—I called each one into my office and broke the news, which they generally took well. Some had a rougher time than others. For example, one guy had to be peeled off the wall. After I relayed to him that I was gay, his body language told me he wanted out of the room. He had no questions, just a desire to end the conversation. Perhaps it had something to do with his Catholic upbringing, but I couldn't get him to open up. He became very distant and guarded.

After a couple years he drifted back into my life. The reason —his older brother, whom he respected and admired, had come out to his family. I think he had begun to realize that just because someone is gay, that doesn't make the person a sexual predator. In fact, we don't chase every man we see—we're just as picky as straight people.

A few years later one of these friends from work asked if I would accept the honor of being the best man in his wedding. My immediate response was, "What will your parents think of you having a gay best man?" He replied, "It's not their wedding." Come to think of it, several straight friends over the years have asked that I be in their wedding parties, which demonstrates the level of trust that's been developed and the strength of our relationships we've nurtured over the years.

The revelation of being gay didn't impact my working relationships with my colleagues. As a team, we had a major client and a ton of work to do as efficiently and effectively as possible. Last time I checked, sexual orientation had nothing to do with following proper procedures for drilling borings, sampling soil or water, installing wells, generating reports, or negotiating with the client and regulatory agencies.

By the spring of 1990 I was feeling burned out on the job and needed a change. While working for the client had been fun, the internal politics of the consulting firm were taking a toll. Physically, I had gained weight I didn't need, my blood pressure and cholesterol were high, and I was really fatigued.

In March I moved back to Washington State and the Hanford site. Not a hard thing to do, as many of the people I had worked with in the past were still there and eager to have me back. Of course, they still had that form with the question about whether I had any "homosexual tendencies." Not a lot had changed in the few years I was gone.

The major drawback was leaving my life and boyfriend in Los Angeles. I had met and fallen in love with an attractive Japanese-Hawaiian man about my age. After resigning from the job in L.A., I stayed with him in Camarillo for a month. We enjoyed our time together, and I had the opportunity to try and sway him to join me in Washington. He had lived in Washington before and shared no desire to move with me.

For the entire month, I slept in, read the paper, worked out, took a run, and spent the afternoons lying on a beach in Ventura. My boyfriend would come home from work and we'd have dinner. During the evenings and the weekends we were together I'd try to convince him to come with me, but to no avail.

When the day came to say good-bye I was starting to feel and look better, but I hadn't made any progress on getting Mike to move. He was doing well at his job and didn't want to quit and move away from family. We had no choice but to end the relationship. Mike was the most difficult part of my life in L.A. to walk away from. But in 1990 the general public still wasn't taking the concept of same-sex relationships seriously, and obviously neither was I. My career was still more important to me than the man I loved. So I packed the last of my things in the SUV and kissed Mike a tearful good-bye.

Life at Hanford was as it had been when I left, with one modest change. Instead of characterizing the site for placement of a nuclear waste dump, we were chartered with cleaning up the site's historical environmental legacy. There was no one in the workplace or friends in the community at the time to whom I felt obligated to come out. I picked Hanford because the assignment was challenging and I'd have time to think through what I wanted to do next with my life.

By leaving Los Angeles, I didn't cut the proverbial umbilical cord and run. I had friends and developed relationships which I continued to nurture and build. Among those friendships was one with a Shell project manager. Turned out his family hailed from the Seattle area. During one of his trips up we decided to meet at the Grants Brewery in Yakima, Washington and catch up over lunch.

We had a great lunch, which actually extended to dinner before we were done. He shared that Shell was looking for someone with my qualifications to join the group in Anaheim, California.

This was the opportunity of my dreams, but having just changed jobs, I was reluctant to tell my employer something better had come along and I was leaving. Over dinner I told him it wasn't a position I'd be interested in because I was settling into a new assignment.

The next morning was a different story—I think the beer wore off. I woke up wanting to kick myself for not having shown more interest in the Anaheim job. This was the chance I'd always dreamed of, and I was turning it away. Finding a bit of courage, I called the project manager and told him that after thinking it over, I wanted to put my name in the hat and try for the job.

Never in my life have I seen a recruiting process move so quickly. I had called the project manager on a Friday morning. Within the hour someone from Shell in Houston wanted a resume, a fax number where he could send some forms, an address for shipping plane tickets, and my availability to travel. By the end of Friday all the forms had been completed and faxed, along with a copy of my resume. Saturday morning the plane tickets arrived. Sunday I was flying to Houston, Texas. Monday was the interview, and that afternoon I flew home.

A few days later, while I was out in the middle of the Hanford desert on a balmy 105-degree afternoon, a colleague and I were trying to get a water pump working when the mobile phone rang. The call was from Shell wanting to communicate a job offer, so I got in the cab of the truck, rolled up the windows and literally sweated it out. After thinking it over for a couple of days, I called back to accept the position.

The prospect of returning to Los Angeles was exciting. A couple of weeks after I accepted the offer, the movers arrived, packed my stuff and took it back to California. I settled in Placentia, a small middle-class community adjacent to Fullerton, only a few minutes' drive to the office in Anaheim. As in the past, I chose not to live in a predominantly gay neighborhood. Believing that perception is everything, I didn't want to give people a reason to speculate about my sexual orientation.

I was hoping to resurrect my relationship with Mike, but a lot had changed in the six months since our tearful departure. He had met another guy and was in the process of settling down with him. In addition to the new job, it looked like I'd also be doing the dating thing again.

That fall of 1990 marked the five-year anniversary of my professional career in the closet. I started the job with Shell in October, becoming the first regional hydrogeologist brought into their marketing organization in the west. The territory was essentially everything west of the Rockies, including Hawaii. I know, rough duty. I knew most of the people in my group from my days as a consultant when they had been my clients.

From a career perspective, Shell was a fantastic opportunity, lauded by many of my straight friends, but viewed more cautiously by gay friends. Believing that one should hope for the best and be prepared for the worst, I dove into the challenges and opportunities the position offered, mindful not to bring my personal life into the office any more then I had to.

I was comfortable that I could pass as a straight person in the workplace. After all, I had been trained most of my life on how to behave as a heterosexual. What I wasn't certain of was whether I could keep my personal life out of the workplace. By keeping my personal life at a distance, I believe, I gave the impression to co-workers that I was hiding something. If relationships are important to success in the workplace, I was creating a dynamic that potentially inhibited building effective working conditions for my advancement.

The challenges of keeping my personal life separate from work were becoming significant. A few weeks into the job I found myself with two weeks in Houston, Texas, for a series of meetings. While I was checking into the hotel, a guy walked up to the desk and asked for a bandage for his finger. I glanced over at him, we made eye contact, and it was apparent to me he was gay. I quickly looked back at the receptionist. To my relief, by the time she had given me the room key, he was gone. I walked over to the elevators, only to encounter the guy again. He too was waiting for a lift. We got into the same elevator, I got off on my floor, and he disappeared up to the higher levels of the hotel. Neither of us had spoken a word up to this point.

As I was unpacking and settling into the room, the phone rang. To my surprise, it was the guy from the lobby wanting to know if I would meet him for drinks and dinner. His name was David, and while behind me in the elevator he'd glanced at the room number on the key in my hand. He was interested in getting acquainted. Given his innovative means and having no other option besides room service, I decided to take David up on his offer.

The next day I went off to my meeting. At the end of the day a bunch of us decided to go out for dinner. A couple of the guys were on my floor and we stopped by my room so I could get rid of my briefcase. On the coffee table when we walked in the door were a dozen roses, a box of chocolates, and a note. The note said, "I'll be back at 6:30 pm, wait and we'll have dinner—D." My jaw dropped. The guys began chiding me about the flowers and chocolate, wanting to know who "D" was.

Going into a defensive mode, I told them in a gender-neutral manner that I had met someone when I checked in the day before. The guys assumed I had a date with a woman, understood and went on to dinner without me. The next day word had spread, and I found myself struggling to explain the situation. In a fit of anxiety, it occurred to me that "D" would become Danielle. By changing just the name, I wouldn't have to change the details of the story. So I told them about Danielle, whom I'd met while checking into the hotel. Fortunately, David had checked out that morning, so there was no chance of our running into each other anywhere.

By the following week, things had calmed down. There was a different set of meetings at the same hotel. During one of the sessions a colleague walked up behind me and gave me a Federal Express envelope. It was from David. I began to blush and got very uncomfortable. The person next to me noticed my reaction and asked what was in the envelope and if I was all right. As calmly as possible, I explained it was a report I hadn't expected for review and I was fine. During the break, I went up to the room and opened the envelope, only to find a Valentine's Day card from David and a pair of white silk boxers with little red hearts. I was so glad I hadn't opened that envelope in the meeting room.

I wasn't sure where Shell was as a company with the topic of sexual orientation when I hired on. One of my first experiences with my peers was on a business trip to San Francisco shortly after starting the job. One evening after dinner, on the way back to the hotel, my colleagues had decided to take a spin through the Castro, a predominantly GLBT neighborhood in San Francisco, to see some of the "nightlife" of the city. I was shocked by the behavior of my colleagues—yelling profanities, crude jokes, and insults.

Not wanting to draw any attention to myself, I just sat quietly in the back seat, subjected to derogatory comments directed at the GLBT community as we drove around. For about half an hour I listened to what my colleagues really thought about the GLBT community as they shouted from the car windows. I was relieved when we finally made it back to the hotel, wanting to be alone to gather my thoughts. The whole situation made me realize that my co-workers only knew the GLBT community based on what they saw on the streets at night. There were no professional role models they could relate to, and based on their behavior, I wasn't about to try to become one.

Later I found out that Shell was actually being sued for discrimination against an employee who was gay. In 1991 a jury ruled in favor of an employee of a Shell subsidiary who had been fired for being gay. Being in the closet allowed me to hear fellow employees' opinions on the issue. Most were surprised at the magnitude of the dollars being awarded. While the final settlement was confidential, the newspapers said the awarded settlement and punitive damages were in the range of $5 million.

Coming back from a meeting, I found several of my colleagues standing in the hall talking about a jury having found Shell guilty in the case and awarding millions in punitive damages. As I walked closer, one co-worker made the comment that "for that kind of money I could bop Rick behind the building, turn myself in, sue Shell and retire."

I was caught off guard by the comment and did my best to just brush it off and go on to my office. But internally it hit a nerve. Why had they singled me out as the example? Did they know something, or was it because I happened to be walking toward them? I tried to preoccupy myself with other things, refocusing on work, but it was hard. Was there something I was saying or doing that was tipping them off to my sexual orientation? Why were they paying attention to me anyway?

I also worried about doing my job too well. There was a recognition program within the Shell retail organization at the time called the Laurel Award. Supervisors nominated people quarterly, and the winners and their spouses were given a trip. My colleagues relished the opportunity to win—for me it was horrifying. The last thing I wanted was visibility that might cause my social and professional lives to collide.

I had received bonuses recognizing when I had performed above and beyond the call of duty. The first came in 1991 for steering a project through troubled waters. The second was for developing a popular training course for the environmental engineers. The bonuses had no significant recognition attached to them other than a check and a handshake from my boss. Yet for me they became a calibration for self-assessing whether I was performing well enough without attracting unwanted attention.

For a while I gauged my work performance, trying to keep the level acceptable, but not outstanding. I was happy to let others take the lead on most projects, giving me the opportunity to be a quiet contributor. On the couple of occasions where I did lead an effort, I received the bonuses.

Apparently I wasn't very good at gauging my performance, as eventually a nomination for the Laurel Award came my way. I was shocked upon hearing the news. My first reaction was to think through how I was going to deal with the situation if I won. I could just slack back a bit on performance, hoping it would minimize my chances. Given what I knew of my work environment, coming out wasn't an option. There was just no easy way out of this one. I decided to roll with the punches and deal with things blow by blow. I'd just try to be inconspicuous, hoping the process wouldn't go beyond a nomination.

You can imagine the sense of relief when I found out I didn't win—a deathblow to my career had been averted. But I wasn't completely out of the woods. The remaining dilemma was more like damage control—what to do with a dinner my boss was hosting for the nominees and their spouses/dates.

Fear, anger, defiance and a certain arrogance complicated my decision making for the dinner. I tried getting out of it, but that was a nonstarter. My boss was adamant about my attending and bringing a date. I thought about taking one of my friends who was a girl, and feeling a little defiant, even considered taking my boyfriend. Ultimately I did go alone, preferring the wrath of my boss to creating another charade. I was the only person at the event without someone, and my boss made no issue of it, for which I was grateful.

Looking back, I realized this was one of my earliest acts of defiance. All the games and charades over the years had been taking a toll. I was tired of having to stage my life like scenes in a play, defining the plot, developing a script, rehearsing every event in my mind, and choreographing them to suit the expected outcomes.

Given my initial experiences with the workplace at Shell, I made a conscious decision to stay long enough to bolster my resume and then move on. My personal life outside the company was sufficiently shielded from view by my colleagues. All I needed was about three years and I could look for something else.

There were other antics that played out as well, like the time a dozen roses showed up at the office. Returning from lunch one day with some colleagues, the receptionist in the lobby stopped me because I had a special delivery waiting. When I asked what it was, she pointed at a vase of red roses—I turned almost as red as the flowers. When I got to my office I called the guy who had sent the flowers, making it very clear he was not to do that again.

The receptionist's husband happened to be the maintenance supervisor for the building and was talking to his wife when the roses were brought to my attention. Afterward she shared with me that she had asked her husband what his reaction would be if she sent him roses at work. He replied, "I'd probably get as red and embarrassed as Rick."

Straight guys don't get flowers at the office. Every time something like this came up, it was like a "red alert": shields went up and I began engaging in evasive maneuvers. The longer I stayed in the closet, the harder it was to keep the rest of the world out. It was physically and emotionally draining each time something new came up. It was analogous to having a switch attached to your emotions; going to work—shut them off; coming home—turn them on. Receiving flowers at work was analogous to blowing a circuit breaker.

One of the more traumatic experiences occurred when a boyfriend moved into my apartment. After a few months I had discovered he was off seeing other guys and decided to end the living arrangements. Unfortunately, he liked where he was living and wasn't interested in leaving, or helping with the bills, for that matter. Finally one night it escalated to the point of his threatening me with a kitchen knife.

That was the final straw. The next morning I spoke with the landlord and explained the situation, and he allowed me to move the next day—a workday. In the morning, without anyone knowing what was playing out in my personal life, I took care of all the critical issues for the day and took the afternoon off.

For most of the afternoon I moved my things alone. Some of my gay friends came over after work and helped with the bigger stuff. Finally, about midnight everything was in the new apartment. The next day, feeling very tired, I was back at work, trying not to show any signs of fatigue from the long day before. No one ever knew.

For the first few years of my career, I hopped companies. I stayed in a work environment long enough to build my career and experience before moving on. The work was usually challenging and the people enjoyable to team with on projects, but there were always comments about gay people and experiences that portrayed the work environment as intolerant. This weighed heavily on my mind for a number of reasons:

- I had formed a perception that being out at work was detrimental to my career. Given the jokes and comments made in the office, I was concerned about being isolated by my peers, or set up for failure.

- Coming out is a transition process that can take years. Changing companies and finding a consistent level of intolerance only made beginning the transition more daunting.

- Conventional measures portrayed a valued employee. Yet they weren't accurate. With each new project I carefully weighed the options, trying to assure my work would be noticeable, but not often recognized as outstanding. Teams were a great place to hide. Contributions could be easily buried in the guise of the group effort put forth.

- As my social world expanded, the task of keeping it separate from my work life became more difficult. An incredible amount of personal energy and concentration were required for me to keep the two worlds from colliding.
- In the workplace I had to be stoic—I couldn't share with colleagues what was happening in my life outside the office. I made a conscious effort to bottle up my emotions and feelings, sometimes not very successfully.

My performance had been sufficient so that in the spring of 1994 I was offered a transfer to the Shell Westhollow Technology Center in Houston, Texas. This was a big move. I'd be relocating into the deeply conservative South. Houston was a city I'd visited in the past, and the relocation would be like starting all over again. Many of my GLBT friends had thought I was crazy when I took a job with Shell in the first place. After hearing about the transfer to Houston and realizing I was going to accept, they knew I was crazy.

My attitude about Houston was different—I viewed what was a great opportunity as a prison sentence. My career was driving change that my life had nothing to do with. I loved California and wanted to stay. I had found some really wonderful friends, but my career called, which meant packing up and leaving it all behind. Allowing myself to be the victim, I quietly accepted the opportunity and began the relocation process.

About this same time, Leona Helmsley made the news, being sentenced to do time for tax evasion. As the story goes, she was rumored to have spent her last few days before serving her sentence at the Ritz Carlton, Laguna Nigel. The prospect seemed very appealing, so I scheduled my last weekend in southern California at the same Ritz Carlton. I could see why someone would go there—the bluffs overlooking the ocean and the peaceful morning walks on the beach really helped frame the beginning of the next phase of my career.

3 The Fork in the Road: Coming Out

Relocation to Houston went smoothly. May was a great time to move—sunny days, cool breezes—quite a contrast to the coming summer months. I found an apartment on the west side of town. The Shell Westhollow Technologies Center was a short 20 minutes further west, a sprawling campus employing about 1,200 people, mostly scientists, engineers, and technicians. These were the people thinking up ways to improve the company's operational and environmental performance.

Upon arrival I was assigned to the Soil & Groundwater Group in the Environmental Directorate. My new responsibilities were mostly in parts of the country other than the West Coast, working with the retail environmental engineers on the East Coast, a refinery and chemical plant outside of New Orleans, and pipelines in the Midwest. These assignments were broadening opportunities, providing experience and exposure to parts of the business operations not previously accessible from a regional position in Anaheim.

If I had to pick a place to come out at work, Westhollow wouldn't be my first choice. While I was in the transition to Houston, I heard that the manager of the Soil & Groundwater Group came to work one day sporting an earring. He was a somewhat eclectic character, and the conversations in the halls varied from him pulling a practical joke to people questioning his sexual orientation. The senior hydrogeologist even went so far as to say, "If a hydrogeologist comes in wearing an earring, I'm going to kick his ass." Hearing this from a person with influence over my career development opportunities just reinforced my resolve not to be out.

By fall I was really missing my friends in Southern California and decided to take a little time off for a visit. They wanted to know how the job was going. They all thought being openly gay in Shell would probably be a really bad career decision. Yet in the back of my mind the timer was still ticking on how long I'd be in the closet. The end of my ten-year self-imposed time in the closet was just around the corner, barely a year away, and I realized I could very well be working for Shell when the time was up.

Having been with the company four years, and in Houston only a few months, it was difficult for me to assess how the workplace culture might react to an openly gay person. I was sure the news wouldn't be well received, but I couldn't gauge the potential impact on my career. Not having any openly GLBT employees in Shell gave the impression to some that the company had no GLBT workers. I knew other GLBT employees existed, but they likely also had the perception that the workplace was too hostile to risk coming out. I really wanted to test the water to get a better sense of the level of tolerance.

One day while vacationing in L.A. and shopping with friends at the Brea Mall, we came upon an earring shop. I'd always wanted an earring but thought it would be troublesome at work. Then it occurred to me—this would be the test. I remembered the response to my boss's sporting an earring for a couple of days in the office. I wanted to know how they would react to someone wearing one all the time. The worst they could do was to have me take it out. So into the shop we went, and a few minutes later I was sporting a gold stud.

Back in the office, even something as small as a gold stud quickly caught people's attention. While most said nothing at all, others either liked it or hated it. Having sported a clip-on earring for a couple of days, my boss thought it was great. The senior hydrogeologist didn't kick my ass, but cautioned me against wearing it when meeting with clients as they might find it offensive.

The biggest lesson for me was the level of tolerance displayed by my co-workers regardless of whether they liked or disliked a guy wearing an earring. The earring was just a very simple change in my appearance—I was gauging my co-workers' comfort level with change. One would expect that a technologies center with a charter that drives change and innovation would be more tolerant than other parts of the business.

A few weeks later, while visiting service station sites with my Florida counterpart, I got a taste of what the senior hydrogeologist was alluding to. While driving between sites, our conversation drifted onto the topic of the GLBT community. In my colleague's mind, gay people were the same as pedophiles, rapists, and alcoholics, and he stated as much. I had chosen not to wear my earring during the workday, mindful of the senior hydrogeologist's advice about clients.

I really resented my colleague's views and didn't want to just brush them off. A passive response seemed appropriate, as I wasn't about to out myself to someone I considered to be homophobic on his turf. So the next day I showed up at my colleague's office wearing the gold stud in my left ear. He said nothing, but from his body language I could tell he didn't like it. I found myself quite comfortable with his discomfort.

The event marked another change in my attitude toward the opinions of others. I was beginning to draw a line in the sand and express my intolerance toward bigotry, but wasn't completely ready to expose myself directly to the prejudice others harbored for the GLBT community. For now it sufficed to have them "bite their tongues."

A couple of days later, while in New Orleans, I had a little time one afternoon to check e-mails before catching a plane to Houston. As I scrolled through the notes, I came upon one from my boss about a co-worker, Nelson, who was leaving the company. The message said he was going on disability, planning to finish a book he was co-authoring on HIV/AIDS.

I was captivated by the e-mail. Completely surprised by the content, I caught myself reading it over and over, searching for something between the lines. Nelson was the project lead for one of the locations I was assigned to support. Being in his office was uncomfortable for me because I found myself attracted to him. I assumed Nelson was heterosexual, but I couldn't stop staring at him. To prevent any embarrassment I tried to minimize our face time, preferring to correspond via phone or e-mail.

I pondered what to do with the e-mail—erase it and go on with life, or reply and potentially open myself up to scrutiny. After a long, agonizing internal debate, I replied, asking my boss if he could offer more details about Nelson. He responded back, asking me to stop by his office.

I didn't want to stop by my boss's office for a conversation; I wanted something more impersonal, like an e-mail. E-mails can hide emotions, but office conversations don't allow that luxury. A conversation in my boss's office might require divulging my sexual orientation to him. I didn't feel ready to do this. While the notes from my boss suggested he was sympathetic and supportive of Nelson, I had no idea how he might react to my being gay. After all, Nelson had left, and in my mind that made the situation easier for my boss to address.

Upon returning to the office, I went to see my boss. Putting on my best "poker face," I asked for more news about Nelson. I started the conversation with questions about how Nelson's work would be reassigned and his last day in the office. My boss shared that Nelson had already left and was reluctant to talk to anyone from work. He acknowledged Nelson was gay and had been diagnosed HIV-positive some years prior. His T-cells were dropping, and Nelson felt a need to change his priorities in life.

More than anything, I wanted to talk to Nelson. For the first time in my career with Shell, I had found another gay person, only to learn about his sexual orientation after he had left the company. I asked my boss how I could contact Nelson to talk about the transitioning of his projects. My boss rather tersely replied that there was no reason for Nelson and me to chat and made clear in his tone that Nelson really wanted to be left alone.

That pissed me off! There was no way this "breeder" was going to stand between me and the opportunity to meet the only other gay employee I had encountered so far in Shell. Finding courage derived from my anger and not being in a polite or diplomatic mood, I told my boss to sit down, shut up and listen.

In confidence I shared my secret. I further stated that Nelson was the only other gay person I was aware of in the company, and I wanted to speak with him. My boss was stoic. After what felt like an eternity absorbing the words, my boss agreed to call Nelson and explore whether he'd be interested in talking with me. I didn't know how to interpret his calmness—was my career in jeopardy, or was he okay with what I had just shared? Was he really going to call Nelson, or would he call HR and arrange for me to be escorted off site?

As I walked down the hall, the full effect of what had just transpired began to sink in—what had I just done? In a fit of anger I had just come out to my boss. All I could think about was the potential consequences of the conversation. Back in my office I really struggled to concentrate on work. Having a plane to catch, I decided to grab my backpack and head off to the airport. Planes have always been a good place for me to think.

Whether I liked it or not, the process of coming out in the workplace had begun. Telling my boss I was gay set the stage for coming out in an environment I viewed as potentially unsafe. Sure, I had gotten a taste of how people might react to something different by wearing an earring, but having a gay co-worker was an amplified difference in my mind.

Arriving at the hotel, I checked voicemails—there was one from my boss. He said Nelson wanted me to call and provided a phone number. Nelson and I later met over coffee. We were both surprised at the discovery of each other's sexual orientation. Having been at Westhollow a few years, Nelson had a good lay of the land and shared his thoughts and insights about people and where their level of tolerance was calibrated.

I described to Nelson the conversation I had had with our boss and his calm reaction. Nelson shared that the way the boss had appeared in the room wasn't what came across in their phone conversation—he seemed more frantic and in a panic. We both agreed the experience would be good for his leadership development. One thing was very clear to Nelson—our boss would definitely be an ally to me in the workplace if I chose to come out.

I think there were a few reasons why my boss was supportive. The overall driver was a company initiative to create learning leaders who grew and developed by stepping out of their comfort zones. I had demonstrated the courage to share something I felt could ruin my career—he seemed to respect that strength. My boss thrived on opportunities to be proactive and lead on tough issues. He also wasn't known for his interpersonal skills, and this was a chance to demonstrate through courage and action that he did value others and could be empathic.

A couple of things resonated for me through our conversations—leadership within the Environmental Directorate would be supportive, and I wasn't the only gay person in the Environmental Directorate. Nelson had shared his perception that there were others, but none would be willing to out themselves to me or anyone else. Whatever I chose to do going forward, I would have supporters among the leadership, but I would be going it alone.

Ultimately, Nelson felt it was important I come out at work, and this was his recommendation to my boss. It was easier for coworkers to deal with Nelson's situation because he had left. I, on the other hand, was still there—they would have to "suffer" my presence, a daily reminder that not everyone neatly fits into society's fabricated norms.

Nelson and my boss agreed to be coaches, helping me maneuver a process I couldn't really comprehend at that juncture. The first thing I had to remind both of them was that they were playing with my life and future, and if I was going to do this, it would be on my terms.

I needed some sense of a plan or road map. My boss thought the best thing to do was to call a meeting of the Environmental Directorate (about 100 people at the time) and just put it on the table. In his mind management would be present, we could all talk through my situation, have some open dialogue and debate, and life would go on. That was a really scary proposition. The thought of standing up in front of a hundred people to tell them I was gay and then deal with their reactions was petrifying. I understood his reasoning—get the issue out there and work with it as a group. But I didn't feel he had a real sense of what I was struggling with —after all, it wasn't going to be him on the front line. While he seemed reasonably comfortable with the topic of sexual orientation, I don't think he realized he was the exception and not the norm.

I proposed a more "organic" approach—no big department meeting, but starting by telling each of the other hydrogeologists and some of the engineers, scientists, and technicians I worked with on a regular basis. I'd give them the opportunity to react and ask questions. This approach was much more manageable and gave me more control over building a base of support. Basically, it was a similar strategy to the one I had used several years earlier when I came out to my straight friends.

The Westhollow leadership team and Human Resources (HR) would be kept appraised of my progress. Preliminary conversations suggested they were supportive, and I felt some sense of relief in knowing this in advance. As for timing, I was ready to begin one-on-one conversations with a list of key colleagues, beginning on National Coming Out day. It was only a few days away and seemed like an appropriate occasion.

I had invested significant effort into mentally and emotionally preparing for the day, being coached and lying awake nights staring at the ceiling, asking myself over and over why I was subjecting myself to all this stress, anxiety, and possible humiliation. The answer came in pieces, which I eventually pulled together.

- I was tired of living a two-faced existence. The mental and emotional drain of this dual existence had taken a toll over the years, and I wanted peace of mind.
- There were other gay people in the workplace like me, and I wanted the opportunity to meet them. I wanted a support network of people who were like me.
- The only way to change attitudes and stereotypes toward the GLBT community was to be a visible role model in the workplace.
- Change wasn't going to happen until someone found the courage to confront the issues and start the process.

The day before, everything was ready to go, and then came a call from my boss saying, "Hold your horses! I met someone you need to speak with before going forward." The person in question was the head of Shell's medical group. Not having a clue as to the reason for the hasty last-minute delay, I agreed to postpone coming out for a few days and paid the good doctor a visit.

Over the course of a two-hour conversation, the doctor probed my thinking and reasoning for coming out. I think he was assessing the breadth and width of considerations to assure everything had been thought through. After our conversation I felt more confident I had a rational plan in place. Nothing we talked about changed my mind; if anything, it reinforced my resolve that this was the right thing to do.

The doctor then introduced me to another person in his department, an openly gay employee in the medical group. The employee was very helpful, lending his perspective and broadening my understanding of how Shell might receive openly gay people in the workplace. I began to realize that the workplace at Westhollow was more the exception then the rule. Corporate HR was not an organization supporting or encouraging diversity and inclusion at the time. There wasn't an interest in adding sexual orientation to the company nondiscrimination policy, nor was anyone exploring whether to offer health benefits to an employee's same-sex partner. Both the employee and the doctor offered their support and wanted to be kept apprised of my progress, which I agreed to do.

After the meeting I called my boss, relaying that nothing had changed. I was ready to come out. We agreed to wait until the coming Monday so he would have time to update the Westhollow leadership team and HR.

With coaches in place, leadership on board, and Westhollow HR ready to respond, one thing was painfully clear—I was still alone. I wasn't seriously seeing anyone. Each night I'd go home and second-guess myself on whether this was the right decision. I was reminded of a dream—I was walking up behind a warrior wearing centurion armor, his long dark locks flailing about his shoulders. He stood on a great prairie facing a cold harsh wind and dark sky. He was alone—no one stood with him as the impending storm approached. It was painfully clear no one would be by my side. I would go home each day to an empty apartment. There would be no arms to hold me or to fall asleep in.

With the stage set, the orchestra had begun to play, and very soon thereafter the curtain would rise. The night before coming out, I lay in bed and thought about all the critics. Like any premier, coming out could be a great success, or a dismal failure. It all hinged upon my commitment to the part. How's that for melodramatics?

The tough part was getting up the courage to tell my peers, and on October 17, 1994, I did just that. I started with a colleague who seemed to be the most homophobic. He had been in the car that night in San Francisco four years prior, and he was the guy who had threatened to kick some ass if anyone showed up with an earring. To my surprise he took the news pretty well, advising that being out at Westhollow was one thing, but I should reconsider how to handle the news with my clients—again advising they might not be as receptive.

Everyone I spoke with seemed to take the news well. The message was simple and clear: 1) I'm tired of hiding the fact that I'm gay and want to be treated with the dignity, respect and professionalism afforded everyone else; 2) If asked about life outside of work, I'd tell them; and 3) If invited to a social function, I might bring a date, which was something they had to get accustomed to or not extend the invitation. Nothing else with regard to my appearance or behavior in the office would differ. I didn't have a boyfriend at the time, so there was no picture showing up on the desk, and I wasn't interested in drawing unwanted attention to myself simply because I was gay.

This may seem like an overly simplistic view of what transpired, but in order for me to do this I needed a script—a crisp first step in the process that could be recited off the top of my head, not be so overwhelming as to cloud my expectations of others, and articulating my desire to be a whole person. I wanted the expectations to be clear and concise so there would be no misunderstanding of my intentions.

I assumed the news would spread quickly to other departments and everyone would know within a couple of weeks. Bad assumption—to my surprise, most considered the information too personal in nature to share with others. I made a bad assumption and quickly realized I shouldn't rely on my colleagues as a distribution vehicle for announcing my coming out. After all, the responsibility wasn't theirs—it was mine. So every day I enlightened a couple more people, and word slowly began to get around.

Throughout the entire ordeal I ran up the phone bill calling close friends, using them as a sounding board and support mechanism. While some disagreed with my decision to come out at work, they were there if I needed them. They offered a voice, if not a physical presence, to help me maintain some sense of sanity.

As more people became aware of my sexual orientation, a sense of isolation began to emerge. While a burden had been lifted from my shoulders, the workplace felt surreal. Others in the department I perceived to be gay kept more of a distance. With few exceptions, even my straight peers would rarely engage in conversation. I was really beginning to think being open with my peers was a bad idea and wrestled with how to undo what I had started.

Then one day I stopped by the department offices to talk with the secretary. Judy Moorad, the environmental director, saw me in the doorway and asked if she could speak with me for a few minutes. She was part of the Westhollow leadership team and had been a silent figure up to this point. While my supervisor and I had had several conversations about what was happening for me in the workplace, Judy and I had had none.

I found her to be very warm and genuinely interested in my well-being. She expressed interest in how things were going since my announcement. Taking a leap of faith, I shared my observations and suspicions, but there really wasn't much in the way of hard data to support what I perceived. She offered an open door and her full support—it was like a small beam of sunlight piercing the darkness.

Judy was someone who recognized the value people brought to an organization. Having lived and worked a portion of her life in the San Francisco Bay area, she had GLBT friends. I think she saw an opportunity to better understand them and their lives by learning from my experiences in the workplace. I think she also realized that if the workplace wasn't inclusive, my productivity would be affected, and that was unacceptable in an organization where people are the primary capital asset.

During the conversation Judy admitted a level of ignorance of the issues for GLBT people in the workplace, as well as a willingness to learn. I was moved by her honesty—too often managers I've encountered seem more willing to bluff their way forward rather than admit a need to learn more on a topic.

At the time I didn't know what the issues were either. I just wanted to come out, live my life, and do my work. All of a sudden a new role seemed to be evolving—educating Judy and other leaders on GLBT workplace issues. But before I could help Judy, I had some learning of my own to do about those issues.

In the days that followed our conversation, I searched websites and hit the GLBT bookstores in search of information on workplace issues. I began identifying and contacting people who were out in other companies who might offer their experiences. Much of my evenings and weekends suddenly seemed fixed on learning about my own community and culture, moving beyond the bars and dance clubs.

Nelson continued to share his experiences and offer what guidance he could. He suggested I meet his boyfriend's roommate, Richard, a former university professor who had left teaching to run Basic Brothers, a men's clothing store in Montrose. So on Halloween, surrounded by the festivities on Pacific Street, I met Richard. He was an older gentleman in his 50s who hadn't lost his zest for life in spite of bearing the burden of being HIV-positive.

As we talked, Richard shared his interests in GLBT workplace issues. Nelson had told him I had just come out, and he seemed genuinely intrigued with how things were going. Richard was very well connected in the Houston GLBT community. Wanting to help, he offered to lend me some material on workplace issues he had in his office at the store.

At the time I didn't fully appreciated what Richard brought to the table in the way of experience, mentoring, and leadership. He used his inquisitive nature to shape and hone my thinking. Eventually, key workplace issues began to materialize: creating a safe work environment where everyone has the opportunity to achieve his or her full potential; adding sexual orientation to the company nondiscrimination policy; creating a support network for GLBT employees and friends; and pursuing domestic partner benefits.

A clearer picture of how Shell was perceived by the GLBT community was also beginning to crystallize. Nelson had given me a book he thought useful, *The Corporate Closet.* While perusing the book, I discovered a footnote referencing the discrimination lawsuit against Shell I had heard about several years prior. The message to the GLBT community was pretty clear—Shell was a company that discriminated against GLBT employees.

I shared everything I learned with Judy. I think she appreciated having the full perspective on the issues and a balanced understanding of what Shell had been doing right and wrong. We both realized the lawsuit was out there—it was part of the current reality, and the past can't be changed. We could only influence the future.

I also shared my thoughts on the major workplace issues. Creating a safe workplace meant a need for an education component. Changing the nondiscrimination policy and adding domestic partner benefits were really policy issues. The concept of a GLBT employee network presented a potential resource to achieve the latter, create a support structure and explore community outreach.

In addition to understanding the issues, Judy also wanted to know how she could be more visibly supportive of me and send that message to others. While doing my research, I had come across a book, *A Manager's Guide to Sexual Orientation in the Workplace,* which I gave her. The book was very helpful in providing case studies of others who had come out in the workplace, as well as lists of things for managers to consider doing to demonstrate their support for GLBT employees.

The holidays were quickly upon us, with office gatherings for both Thanksgiving and Christmas. None of my colleagues had extended invitations to holiday parties or for drinks after work, so I made do by hanging out with my gay friends.

My first opportunity to bring a date to a company function didn't occur until a couple of months into the new year. In an effort to get to know each other better, Judy arranged a dinner gathering at a Houston restaurant that was open to spouses and significant others. This was the first time I had seen the words "significant others" included in an invitation. This wasn't by chance; Judy had wanted the invitation to be more open and inclusive of everyone, including me.

The first question for me was, should I even go? I wasn't dating anyone at the time and could go by myself, which would have been the easy answer. It would certainly alleviate any discomfort for others not used to seeing a gay couple in public. Yet the right answer isn't always the easy answer. I was tired of going to events by myself. The only way people ever become comfortable with something is by facing their discomfort and understanding the root causes. I've found my discomfort with situations or groups is often caused by stereotypes and societal prejudices rather than personal experiences and solid data. In order for me to do my part toward educating other people, I felt an obligation to attend and take a date.

The next question was who to take. Over the holidays I had met a guy named Oscar who worked for Richard at Basic Brothers. He wasn't seeing anyone at the time. I shared with him my anxiety over whether to attend the dinner. The reality was that we probably wouldn't feel comfortable. In fact, we might be sitting alone. In spite of my landscape of trepidation, Oscar agreed to be my date for the dinner.

The night of the dinner we were both pretty nervous. While we made it to the restaurant, neither of us seemed to have the courage to walk into the dining room. Leaving actually seemed like a better solution than facing the unknown. In order to calm down, Oscar and I did a quick detour into the bar, where I ordered a couple of shots of whiskey. After a quick toast to a safe and enjoyable evening, we downed the shots and headed in to dinner.

The managers were the first to greet us when we entered the room. Others soon followed. When the time came to be seated, Oscar and I took a table where no one else had yet been seated. This was my way of graciously allowing others in the room to decide whether they wanted our company for the evening. It was also an opportunity for me to gauge where I might find support among my peers. After what seemed like an eternity, but was really only a few minutes, others joined us—I doubt they knew how relieved we were to have the company.

Everyone at the table made Oscar and me feel welcome. Among them were Judy and her husband, who could have sat anywhere in the room, but chose our table. At that point I realized Judy was sincere about her commitment of support—it was all the tangible evidence I needed.

The evening came and went without incident. Oscar enjoyed meeting my co-workers, and they seemed to like him. The event brought out an important lesson—whether I liked it or not, I was becoming a role model in the workplace. People's perceptions were influenced that night by the behaviors Oscar and I exhibited during the dinner.

After the dinner event I felt more self-confident. This feeling seemed to be propagated by the tolerance of my peers toward an openly gay employee and the tangible support of leaders in my department. I began reevaluating my coming out process, wanting to push the envelope further.

Initially I had decided not to come out to my clients. Now as a next stage, I began thinking about other stakeholders with whom I worked. In addition to my clients in the business, there were peers in other companies, law offices, and a number of consulting firms. I decided to selectively bring clients into the circle, wanting to build a network of people who would be supportive in the event others down the road had problems working with someone who was gay. When it made sense, I would also enlighten the law firms and consultants with whom I worked.

Bringing these others on board wasn't easy. At times there were complications to be managed. As an illustration, a series of events played out on an EPA Superfund site in Nevada. I was assigned to the project when it began in early 1991 while I was on the West Coast. Prior to transferring to Houston, I participated on a team with peers from other oil companies, which set into motion a series of events intended to break a legal logjam. Upon transferring to Houston, I left the project behind. Several months later the events I'd helped set into motion achieved the desired outcome, and there was an elevated interest among the parties to reach settlement through mediation.

After a nine-month absence I found myself reassigned to the project as the technical lead on the Shell mediation team. The team was comprised of the business manager, engineer, inside and outside counsel, and myself. I'd really enjoyed being part of the team. Most members knew I was gay and really didn't care.

With the impending mediation came document requests, which included my work journals, the very place I had made references to my coming out process in Shell. It may seem odd to make reference in the journals to my coming out process, but these were the books in which I calendared all of my meetings and captured voicemails that needed to be returned. So meetings and calls with management and Human Resources related to coming out at work and the follow-up meetings were all in the journals.

While my sexual orientation wasn't an issue for the Shell team, I was concerned that other companies with more liability at stake might see a way of using the information to their advantage, potentially challenging my character if the case went before a jury. I met with our attorneys on the case and explained my concerns. The outside counsel agreed to keep the relevant work journals in their offices. I went through all the affected volumes and flagged any references to the case. The attorneys agreed that should any of the other parties want to see the entries, they would be allowed to review only those pertaining to the case. What I appreciated most was the attorneys' not seeing my sexual orientation as a catastrophe, but rather as an issue to be worked out in the context of the case, a minor issue.

During most of 1995 I was heavily preoccupied with the case. In spite of my workload and travel, I continued to make time for GLBT workplace issues. A strategic team had been established by Shell leaders with the charter of studying diversity and making recommendations on how the company might proceed in this area. During the spring of 1995, they commissioned a consultant to interview a cross section of employees to provide a picture of current reality. I stumbled onto the interviews during a hallway conversation with a Hispanic colleague who was approached by the consultants to participate in the interviews.

With this little piece of knowledge, I spoke with Judy, who in turn made some calls. Not wanting to be the only gay person interviewed, I also called the gay employee in Medical. I had also asked that Nelson be included even though he was no longer with Shell. Our interviews were over the phone, focusing on what we perceived as the current state of the workplace for gay employees. From debriefs with Nelson and the employee in Medical, I learned we had all emphasized the need for some assurance that discrimination on the basis of sexual orientation would not be an acceptable workplace behavior.

That same year another book, *Cracking the Corporate Closet,* looked at how tolerant different industry sectors were for GLBT employees. The chapter on the oil and gas industry was less then flattering. The only fully integrated oil company to complete the survey for the authors was Chevron. Shell was among a host of companies not responding to the survey request. Given the lack of any other information, the authors searched the public record and subsequently developed the Shell summary, which focused on the California lawsuit that had been settled in the early 1990s.

The reoccurring presence of the lawsuit, the only tangible record of the company's behavior toward its GLBT employees, was a constant reminder of the reality of the workplace. This book went a step further by establishing a context for the industry, as well as Shell, neither of which invited a warm, embracing appeal. After reading the chapter, it seemed clear that the word on the street was to steer away from the oil and gas industry if you were looking for a tolerant workplace.

In my little microcosm of the company, the rootlets of acceptance were becoming visible, with most people expressing some degree of tolerance. The story could have been much different if not for the support of management. If people were having trouble working with me because of my sexual orientation, they weren't saying anything to me.

As Judy and my supervisor became more comfortable with the workplace issues, they used their knowledge, interjecting their thoughts into the process of evaluating the need for diversity in Shell. Judy vicariously saw through me what life in the workplace was like for someone who was gay. She also saw what life would be like if she weren't lending her support to creating an equitable workplace. Others were also dropping by her office to share their desire for Shell to be a "Christian" company displaying Christian values.

While Judy was my coach and mentor in the workplace, Richard was filling a similar role outside the company. We met frequently over dinner or at his house over a glass of wine. Having a background in education, Richard was an effective mentor and coach. His guidance reinforced that I needed to remain patient and be a role model.

As much as I enjoyed learning from Richard, I enjoyed learning about him too. He had left teaching years earlier, entering the clothing business with his partner at the time. After losing two partners to HIV/AIDS, he really wasn't looking for another. Richard had also acquired HIV/AIDS and knew I was afraid of the virus gnawing at his body. Our conversations about the virus made me very uncomfortable, and he helped me realize that for him to be an effective teacher, I had to conquer my fear.

This was my second lesson in facing something I feared—the first having been coming out. With Richard's help I learned more about HIV/AIDS. He often referred to his illness as a gift—something that helped him to focus on the importance of life. At the time "cocktails" of medication weren't yet commercially available. Richard's doctor was trying to get him into some of the trials, but his T-cell count was marginal.

Knowing he didn't have long to live, Richard spent his days making time for his daughter and a new grandson, making Basic Brothers operations reasonably self-sufficient, supporting various community projects, and putting his life in order. He definitely wasn't about to call it quits and watch his time slowly pass. He really felt there was too much yet to accomplish in spite of the time limitations.

As part of my learning process I made a personal commitment to visit Richard whenever he was in the hospital, and in 1995 he was in and out a lot. I've long considered hospitals the antithesis of life—gloomy, sterile institutions that seem to strip people of their dignity. No offense to hospitals, but it's my "baggage" and I'm stuck with it. The hospital Richard used was actually close to where I lived, so every day when he was there I would leave work, pick up some magazines or a newspaper and drop by for a visit.

Watching the nurses and doctors taking care of Richard, meeting some of his family and friends, and just talking during our visits helped me immensely in overcoming my fears. I learned to respect the virus that had invaded his body and not let it interfere with the development of our mentoring relationship.

From our many conversations I realized a need to become more involved in my community to really understand the issues and how they were being worked on. Richard suggested that an effective vehicle might be my participation on the board of a few GLBT nonprofit groups. In my mind one of the boards had to be with a HIV/AIDS organization to help me further my learning, and another with an organization focused on the GLBT business community.

Nelson had completed his book on a program to inhibit loss of body mass associated with HIV/AIDS. In addition to developing a wellness program for people suffering from the wasting effects of HIV/AIDS, Nelson was also creating a non-profit organization, Program for Wellness Restoration (PoWeR). Eventually they created a board, and Richard and I were on it.

Later the same year Richard forwarded an invitation for me to become a charter member of the Greater Houston GLBT Chamber of Commerce. The November charter meeting of the GLBT Chamber opened my eyes to the diversity of the business community. Over a hundred people attended the event, representing travel agencies, accounting/financial services, real estate agencies, hotels, retail, publishing, etc. I was amazed at the number of small businesses dispersed in and among the streets and avenues of Montrose and other parts of the city. Through PoWeR, the Chamber, and various charity events, Richard provided me a venue for meeting some of the influential leaders in the Houston GLBT community, and others who were working in Houston's corporate offices.

My level of trust with Richard had grown dramatically over that first year. To help him develop a better understanding of my thoughts and ideas, I decided to share with him some of my personal diary. The diary was a place where I could think on paper. Some people need to speak to articulate views, thoughts, ideas, and feelings. I needed a safe place to write them.

Richard was very surprised when I showed up on his doorstep with a printed version of my diary. He promised to read the entire book, a task I thought would probably take a couple of weeks. To my astonishment, he sat down the next day and read the whole thing over a period of several hours. In addition to learning about those things dear to me, he also came upon a revelation—I should write.

I began journaling in a diary format as a freshman in high school. Writing provided the outlet for reasoning through all the stuff cluttering my mind, essentially the board on which the pieces of the puzzle all lay. The thought of writing anything other than a personal diary had not occurred to me, yet Richard felt it was a talent I should explore. With some guidance I became more adept at using my words to maneuver the pieces in my mind, working through how they would begin to fit together. Having only begun the journey of coming out, the picture was not yet known to me—so I began by setting a context for why I had begun the journey.

I was very fortunate to have Richard and Judy enter my life. Had I not come out, I certainly would not have had the opportunity to know either. They were a personally rewarding benefit of being openly gay—I was making progress toward leading one life instead of two, learning about workplace issues for GLBT employees, educating others, influencing policies that affected gay employees, beginning to expand my network of contacts among the leaders of the Houston GLBT community, and taking an active interest in some of the community organizations.

I was becoming more comfortable talking about my social life in the office. I had been able to bring dates to some company functions, and I had helped some of my peers who were wrestling with perceptions of gay culture. Much of the change occurring in the work environment was created by the steadfast support of Judy and my boss. I think some of the reasons contributing to the success so far were these:

- Having a plan and crisp message to relay to colleagues about why I was coming out and what the decision meant in the workplace, revisiting the plan periodically and making modifications where appropriate.

- Realizing that to effectively educate others on workplace issues, I first had to educate myself. Some of the knowledge came from various media and the rest from experiences and involvement in the community.

- Finding mentors like Judy and Richard who influenced my overall development and growth as a leader. With their support I learned to conquer my fears and find the courage to begin stepping out on issues.

- Learning the importance of being an effective role model for the GLBT community and employees in the workplace. Without role models, stereotypes persist.

- Being visible on GLBT issues in the workplace—not as an irritant, but as a resource to help educate management and increase their awareness.

- Realizing that coming out wasn't about standing out—if someone is an exceptional employee, he or she already stands out. I really just wanted to be myself, comfortable in a work environment that allowed me to contribute to my full potential.

- Articulating that I wasn't asking for special privileges because I was different—just the respect, dignity and opportunities offered everyone else.

- Realizing that coming out wasn't over after telling my peers. This is a lifelong journey, which I began on October 17, 1994.

Sure, the company non-discrimination policy had not yet been amended to include sexual orientation, but my being out gave a voice and visibility to an otherwise transparent minority and their view of the workplace.

4 Unimaginable Changes in Life

I had thought the new year would afford me the luxury of time to absorb more information before engaging more leaders. The coming year offered nothing of the sort, just more demands on my time. The more I learned, the more there was to accomplish. The change to the non-discrimination policy was moving along. Through the GLBT Chamber I had the opportunity to meet those in other companies involved in the creation of employee networks. They were a wealth of information on how their companies had reached the decision not to discriminate on the basis of sexual orientation.

Changing the non-discrimination policy may seem trivial to some in this day and age, but for an oil and gas giant, policy changes can occur at a glacial pace. By early 1996 a number of oil and gas companies, including Amoco, Chevron and Mobil, had already established precedence for the industry. While today many in the industry have changed their non-discrimination policies, some still have not. For example, ExxonMobil, the largest integrated oil and gas company in the world, as of this writing still sees no reason for adding sexual orientation to their nondiscrimination policy. After years of shareholder propositions, the company still maintains it does not discriminate and the words aren't necessary. As of this writing, shareholders owning 35 percent of company stock support the policy change.

The Shell approach was quite different. A strategic team on diversity was chartered in 1995 to study the topic of diversity and make recommendations for how an initiative could be leveraged by the company. The drivers for the team desired to increase productivity through creating a more inclusive work environment, better position the businesses to compete globally, maximize the effectiveness of teams, and encourage employees to achieve their full potential. The team was comprised of senior managers, half of whom were women and people of color. Initially, the team members seemed to concentrate on their own learning needs and develop a sense of the workplace in the following ways:

- Evaluating any existing data relevant to the workplace climate.
- Experiencing learning about differences through awareness workshops.
- Applying their discoveries to understanding the dynamics of the workplace culture and the self-perpetuating systems it created.
- Validating and testing their perceptions through interviews with different cross sections of employees and a roundtable discussion with experts in the field of diversity.
- Benchmarking with other companies to better understand their strategies for implementing diversity initiatives.
- Testing their findings with a diverse focus group of people who were comfortable challenging the report and making recommendations.

At the time I learned of the team's efforts, they were in the process of surveying different cross-sections of the employee population. Nelson, an employee in HR, and I were able to participate. As Judy and my boss increased their knowledge and understanding of sexual orientation as a workplace issue, they became more vocal and supportive of changing the non-discrimination policy to include sexual orientation. While neither was on the strategic team for diversity, they both knew and worked closely with some of the members. I shared what I learned with Judy and my boss, making them an effective conduit for sharing the knowledge with the team.

I also had a sense of what other organizations the strategic team for diversity had selected for benchmarking. Many on the list were leaders in their industries and had already added sexual orientation to their non-discrimination polices. My impression was that this helped the cause.

After many months of research and learning, the Strategic Team for Diversity released their final report in January 1996. Among the recommendations was inclusion of sexual orientation in the company non-discrimination policy. Even more exciting was the news of Shell's U.S. leadership team having accepted all the recommendations.

Within a few more months the recommendation to add sexual orientation became a reality. On April 15, 1996, the revised policies were posted in all work locations. This was only one of a host of recommendations, which included establishing a diversity center, hiring a diversity director, and creating a policy and benefits review team. The recommendations of the team were far-reaching. Not only were they changing the policy, they also set in motion the creation of vehicles for potentially tackling domestic partner benefits, creating employee networks, and promoting community outreach.

Judy shared my excitement about the policy change. Later that day I gave Richard an update. I must have been pretty excited, as he just sat there listening to me babble, smiling and giggling with a characteristic twinkle in his eyes. After I finally slowed down, he interjected that the time had come for me to write my coming out story and get it published. The news about the non-discrimination policy change could be a crowning piece.

This was obviously something Richard had had in the back of his mind for a while. He had been encouraging me to do more writing ever since he'd read my diary. Up to that point I hadn't published any articles or books. Richard knew Greg Jue, the publisher of *Out Smart*, a monthly magazine catering to the Houston GLBT community. I met with Greg, who was very interested in the story and also wanted to do a piece on Shell's changing their policy.

I didn't see the appeal of my coming out story, however, and said as much to Richard. He replied, "Writing and publishing your story will change your life in ways you can't even begin to imagine." Now I have a very vivid imagination—just ask any of my friends. Richard had yet to steer me wrong, so taking a leap of faith, I wrote the story.

I gave a lot of thought to what should be accomplished by the article. At first, "I'm here, I'm queer, get used to it" seemed like a good idea. But an article provided the unique opportunity to relay a message. I wanted to be sure it was a message I believed and could stand behind. It had to be crisp—there wouldn't be the luxury of pontificating in a magazine article. The story had to be real—the feelings, emotions, and most importantly, how I would position myself for the journey ahead.

I'd made a personal commitment to keep Judy informed of my progress as I drafted my story. She had been very supportive so far, and I wanted to earn her trust. As a courtesy I forwarded the final draft to her before it went to the magazine. Her only request was that I share the piece with Shell media relations in the spirit of open communication.

Media relations was new territory for me—I just wanted to write a good story. I had the perception that media relations was mostly a defensive mechanism for protecting corporate reputation, so I hadn't expected them to be very encouraging or proactive. After providing them a copy of the story, they called to voice support. To my surprise, they seemed genuinely interested in the article, not controlling, just wanting to understand the motivation for creating the piece. For them, the story meant visibility for Shell. They needed the ability to effectively respond to any inquiries, good or bad, that might result. Working together, we came up with a list of potential questions and possible replies.

The article had not even been published and was already offering opportunities for positive exposure. That initial conversation created some common ground upon which Media Relations and I kindled a long-lasting relationship. Over the years our trust and respect for each other grew through collaboration on a number of projects.

Human Resources (HR) had created an internal communication plan for managers to use in briefing employees about the change to Shell's non-discrimination policy, but not an effective implementation strategy. The updated policy and a list of potential questions and answers were sent to managers under a cover letter from HR briefing them on the change. Departments were instructed to post the new policy. Should questions arise, management could choose to answer them or involve their HR representative. Simple enough. What more did they need?

This was the first time most employees and many managers were hearing the words "sexual orientation" uttered in a workplace context, and there was nothing in the way of formal training to help them understand the ramifications of the change. In my travels to different Shell facilities around the country, I found myself reading bulletin boards to see if the new policy was there. Most employees hadn't noticed the change, and most managers weren't bringing it up—analogous to letting a sleeping dog lie.

Judy took a different approach, using the department staff meeting as a venue to announce the policy change. I happened to be traveling that day, but heard from others that only a couple of people voiced opposition. One person shared that, while he didn't have a problem working with people of color, women, and others, he had a real problem working with homosexuals. Judy's reply was very direct: "If you have a problem working with homosexuals, then I have a problem that needs to be addressed." At that point the employee quickly withdrew his objection as Judy explained that treating people with dignity and respect were expected behaviors in the workplace. She and her leadership team made very clear that this was about changing behaviors in the workplace, not people's beliefs.

Judy was effective in communicating the expectations of the company, a tangible indication of her own learning through our conversations. Yet she was the exception, not the rule—there really were no subject matter experts that employees could talk to if they wanted to learn more. The lack of educational resources for managers and employees was a very apparent weak link.

Soon after the meeting, some of the other GLBT employees in the department became a bit less distant. They weren't going to come out in the workplace, but some were willing to meet up with me after work or occasionally grab lunch off site. Most saw Judy's communication as supportive of an inclusive work environment, but they also wanted to see more before they'd come out.

There was an obvious need for a resource to help managers and employees in their learning about GLBT workplace issues, and a support mechanism for GLBT employees wanting to come out at work. The logical next step seemed like the creation of an employee network, something I had never done before.

All of the work activities pertaining to GLBT workplace issues were in addition to my regular job responsibilities. Some activities and events had to take place during the workday. Initially these activities were minimal, but over time, as more people became involved, the work expanded and I had to strike a balance with my day job. Fortunately my management saw value for the company from my efforts and agreed to support some of them. Still, it was a two-way street; some things the company would cover, but there were other opportunities that I had to follow on my free time.

During my evenings after work and on the weekends, I took on the task of exploring how to build a GLBT employee network. Utilizing and honing my own networking skills through the GLBT Chamber, I discovered that Texas Commerce Bank (now Chase Texas), Amoco (now BP), Exxon (now ExxonMobil), and Chevron (now ChevronTexaco) all had GLBT employee groups. Learning from the Strategic Team for Diversity, I began doing my own benchmarking on GLBT employee networks.

Through conversations with the leadership of these networks, I discovered that they varied with regard to structure, focus and success. Some had a single chairperson, while most had co-chairs. Most were governed by steering committees ranging from six to twelve employees. While some were formally recognized and financially supported by the company, others were not. They were tackling a variety of challenges: company recognition of their employee network, education, adding sexual orientation to the non-discrimination policy, growing their membership, exploring outreach opportunities for their employers in the GLBT community, and acquiring domestic partnership benefits.

Their ability to move on these issues seemed directly tied to how strong their relationships were with senior leadership in the company. Most had access to company facilities for meetings and communication. At the time only one group was denied use of the e-mail system or company facilities. The employee network groups in Houston tended to be analogous to chapters of larger corporate-wide networks.

Through these conversations I began to formulate what a network could look like in Shell. Initially the challenge would be finding a critical mass of people willing to help build the structure. To find a critical mass of people, I first had to find the GLBT community within Shell.

By mid-May 1996 the new edition of *Out Smart* magazine hit the street. I picked up extra copies for distribution to Media Relations, Judy, my boss and others. It seemed odd having my picture and story in print. My whole life I'd shied away from taking a public stand on what I thought. Now my views and perspectives were staring back at me from the pages of a magazine.

The next day something very unexpected happened—e-mails and voicemails began appearing from people in the company who had seen the article. They were the "GLBT underground" of Shell —people I had never met. In all, a couple of dozen sent notes and left voice mail messages.

The unimaginable was happening—there were other people like me in the company, and they were reaching out. I replied to each and every message, wanting to meet each and every person. There were so many questions I wanted to ask—what were their experiences, how were they coping in the company, were there others?

One of the notes was from an employee working at the Shell Wood Creek facility on the west side of town, not far from Westhollow. He'd read the article and was inspired to also come out at work. We shared many e-mails, phone calls and lunches working through his coming out and talking about the next step—creation of a GLBT employee network.

There were some hurdles to getting started. Getting a network organized and off the ground was more work than the two of us could handle. How were we going to structure things? What would be the network's focus? How were we going to build membership? How would we learn about the issues in the workplace? What were we going to communicate?

We needed to muster more support. Enlisting the services of another colleague who had been maintaining a distribution list for an informal group of gay employees called the Lunch Bunch, we did what any three gay men would probably have done in our situation—we decided to throw a party. Cliché, perhaps—effective, definitely!

The party made sense. The story in *Out Smart* magazine and the change to the company non-discrimination policy were sufficient justification for such an event. Our first objective was to bring people together socially in a non-threatening setting. The second objective was to hopefully garner interest among some of those present to participate on a steering team chartered with creating a GLBT employee network. The third was to try and obtain insights of what the workplace was like for Shell's GLBT community and where we should focus the network's efforts.

My colleague from Wood Creek generously offered his home for the event. Others helped with the invitations and planning. We were also busily pulling together a survey. Using resources extracted from the Internet, a two-part survey emerged: the first part solicited perceptions of the state of the workplace for gay and lesbian employees. The second part focused on obtaining information to start a mailing directory, evaluating activities of interest to members, soliciting volunteers for a steering committee, and obtaining ideas for a network name. People would pick up a survey at the party and send them anonymously back to me via company mail marked confidential. We didn't have permission to use the company mail system at the time, but given that the data would shed some insight on life in the workplace for gay and lesbian employees, there was certainly a business context.

The most important reason in my mind for doing the surveys was to bring as many voices as possible into the decision-making process of creating a network. Creating a network was not about two or three people sitting in a room—we needed ways to bring transparency to the process, and surveys were one such method. Results from the survey would hopefully also establish a baseline of the demographics of the group.

The emphasis of the first survey was on the "gay, lesbian, and bisexual" communities of Shell. The transgender community had been initially neglected because of ignorance on our part—we didn't know anyone in the company who was transgender at the time. This was an unfortunate oversight that was eventually corrected.

The party went off without a hitch. About seventy people showed up for the event, including employees and their partners/dates. An hour into the evening we all crowded into the living room, where I shared thoughts on the significance of the party and the surveys.

Over the next couple of weeks the surveys began to trickle into my office; by mid-August, thirty-two surveys had been received. I didn't expect there would be many, and I certainly didn't expect them to all come in at once. That said, this was our first glimpse of the experiences of the GLBT community in the company, which was exciting. The survey responses were mainly from the greater Houston and New Orleans areas, where most of Shell's employees were located. Having the insights of thirty-two people from various Shell businesses was something unimaginable just a few weeks prior.

In addition to having people check boxes, we also encouraged them to write comments about the workplace. As I opened the envelopes and sifted through the data, I found that many had taken the time to share their experiences in writing. My challenge was finding time to summarize it all. It hadn't occurred to me beforehand that compiling the results would be time-consuming work.

The only opportunity appeared to be a block of time I had set aside for vacation in early September. I was going up to Idaho to spend a week with someone I had been dating. Most of my days on vacation were spent toiling away on the surveys, and by the end of the week a draft summary report was completed.

The results of the surveys showed that for this pool of respondents, most were in long-term relationships, with the average length being eight years. The participants were well educated, with most having a college degree. Most were male; only two were minorities. Their partners were teachers, computer programmers, restaurant managers, real estate agents, and other professionals.

Some had children. Only three of us were completely out in the workplace.

Throughout the several pages of comments and stories, people shared some common themes:

- Domestic partner benefits were important.
- There was a desire for a safe work environment where everyone was treated with dignity and respect, and not subjected to off color jokes and derogatory comments.
- Others wanted the opportunity to achieve their full potential and not fear that their sexual orientation might be career limiting and negatively impact their compensation.

Another outcome of the survey was a more robust steering committee. Several survey participants expressed interest in the leadership of the network going forward. The team quickly grew from three to six. Just because someone was on the steering team did not mean the person was out at work.

All of the original steering team members were gay men. Some women had attended the party, and we struggled to get their representation on the steering committee. Within a few months, women were a part of the team. People of color were a more elusive group, as so few were part of the initial "word of mouth" group that had come together.

The first issue for the new steering team was coming up with a charter and a name for the network. What may seem a simple task was actually rather arduous. After reviewing all the submissions and with much debate, the team settled on SEA Shell (Support, Equality, Awareness at Shell). The name embodied the purpose for the network and the work it would undertake.

After coming up with a name, the team turned its attention to creating the mission of SEA Shell: *To provide support for members and co-workers, promote equality for employees regardless of sexual orientation, and create awareness in management of issues and concerns affecting people in a diverse workplace.* Originally this mission statement was brought to life by seven goals:

- Promote awareness and education of Shell's staff and management on current issues dealing with sexual orientation.
- Provide the resources to support diversity training that promotes equality for all Shell employees, regardless of sexual orientation.
- Provide support to any Shell employees in situations involving discrimination, harassment, or any other problem associated with sexual orientation in the workplace.
- Explore opportunities for Shell to demonstrate its commitment to the gay and lesbian community in a manner that is consistent with Shell's core values.
- Provide Shell management with the resources to enable them to extend full domestic partner benefits to all employees regardless of sexual orientation.
- Provide an opportunity for its members to network within Shell, and with similar employee groups in other corporations.
- Support Shell's health services organization to develop AIDS awareness training for all employees.

This was a very aggressive roadmap given that only three people were openly gay. The basic components of these goals focused on education, outreach, support and benefits. To achieve these ends would ultimately require more people to be out at work.

From the earliest stages of development, the network realized the need to tie into the basic core values of the company that guided expected behaviors in the workplace. Eventually the seven goals were refined into three, with clear linkages expanding beyond just the core values to include key business strategies for Shell in the U.S.

Next on the agenda was communication—how were we going to correspond as a network, within Shell and with the outside world? A significant challenge was the various levels of comfort people had with receiving SEA Shell e-mails at work. Some people wanted their names hidden, others were okay with their names visibly attached, and a handful didn't want to be on an e-mail distribution at all. To assure some level of consistency in our approach, one member of the steering committee assumed the role of communication officer with another assigned as a backup. Since most of the steering team was from the IT organization, they knew how to conceal names on a distribution list for e-mail correspondence. This appeared to provide a sufficient level of anonymity for people not wanting to be recognized as part of the group. The very few who were not comfortable being on any list were notified of upcoming events via phone calls.

Having different degrees of visibility was manageable, and over time we hoped more people would move to the visible list. SEA Shell social and networking venues, progress on GLBT workplace issues, and support from senior leaders did eventually stimulate the migration of more members to the visible distribution list. As the visible list grew, it became a barometer of a member's comfort level being associated with SEA Shell. Another important point—SEA Shell was not strictly for GLBT employees; straight allies could also join. In the beginning anyone interested in becoming a member of SEA Shell could contact a steering committee member and they were added to the distribution.

Given that employee networks were not sanctioned at the time, a question facing SEA Shell was whether the network could use the Shell e-mail system for communications at all. Judy offered to investigate on our behalf. I provided a draft list of some basic guidelines:

- The system would be used as a communication mechanism for workplace diversity issues.
- The system would be used for scheduling meetings and polling the GLBT community on their opinions on issues of diversity.
- The system would be used for the transmittal of information on corporate policies/procedures relevant to GLBT employees.
- The distribution list would be confidential so as to respect the right to privacy of members and not inadvertently out them to others.

I was surprised afterward to discover that Judy went straight to the CEO with her inquiry. His response was favorable—as long as the system was being utilized for constructively achieving diversity-related objectives supporting the business.

Judy was playing an important role, evolving into a senior management advisor for the network. Helping with the communications barriers and voicing support for changing the non-discrimination policy to include sexual orientation were two early examples of how she was an effective liaison for GLBT employees in helping others understand the issues.

We also wanted to get word about SEA Shell on the street. The primary objectives were to let the GLBT community know that an informal employee group existed, and to provide a vehicle through the GLBT media for other Shell employees not out in the workplace to find out about SEA Shell. SEA Shell was listed with a number of web groups that tracked GLBT workplace issues, and a free ad was placed in *Out Smart* magazine in the community section. These efforts eventually bore fruit and contributed to the growth of SEA Shell.

As the charter for SEA Shell materialized, I assembled an onboarding packet for new members of the fledgling GLBT employee network. The first packets included the mission and goals for SEA Shell, a copy of my coming out story, and the SEA Shell survey. As other documents became available, they were added to the stack. When someone joined SEA Shell, the communications officer would add his or her name to the appropriate distribution list, and I would forward the on-boarding packet. I either delivered the packet in person or sent it stamped "confidential" through the company mail with a note asking to meet the employee.

My personal desire was to meet every one of SEA Shell's members as they came into the network. In addition to making some great friends, it was an opportunity to put a "face" on SEA Shell. People knew me and seemed to prefer directing others to a real person who could tell them about SEA Shell.

Meeting new members also created an opportunity to gather more knowledge about the workplace environment and a sense of the issues employees viewed as important. It was a great way to discover where people were on coming out and what might motivate them to move to the next level. For some it just wasn't going to happen, because they didn't feel the culture of the company was going to really change. For others it was going to take tangible evidence of change, like adoption of DP benefits, Shell's support of GLBT-friendly legislation, or the Shell Oil Company Foundation making contributions to GLBT charities. Knowing some of the triggers for people was helpful in validating the value proposition for SEA Shell.

There was another unexpected consequence from my coming out story. The Environmental Directorate had a bulletin board reserved for posting current publications generated by the researchers in the department. One day while scanning the articles on the board, I was surprised to see my coming out story posted. My first reaction was to take it down, because at the time only a handful of people in the department knew I was gay.

Then I began contemplating the intent of putting my story on the board. One thought was that someone supportive of my willingness to come out felt that others could learn from reading the article. The other side of the coin was that someone posted the article to solicit a backlash that would put department leadership in an awkward position. Whatever the motive, my next stop was Judy's office.

I explained the situation to Judy, who asked how I wanted to proceed. Regardless of intent, I wanted to use the posting of my story positively. The opportunity posed by the posting increased my visibility as an openly gay employee. I recommended to Judy that the article be left on the board and any negative responses be dealt with when and if they came up. Other than a few people expressing their surprise about my sexual orientation, nothing more came of the posting incident.

Just as Judy was a steadfast supporter in Shell, Richard provided inspiration and a backdrop to my community activities. He was someone with whom I could share my excitement, fears, thoughts, frustrations and confusion. It was very fortunate that our paths had crossed, but while his commitment and interest were strong, his health was poor.

During the year he had been in and out of the hospital on numerous occasions. HIV/AIDS was slowly ravaging his body. He barely made it into the early trials for the protease inhibitors, as his T-cell count was very low. Shortly after we met on Halloween in 1994, I realized he could have a profound impact on my life, yet probably wouldn't live to realize the full effect of his influence. That reality hit home during one of his hospital stays when I really thought I would lose him.

A friend called to tell me Richard was in the hospital and it looked quite serious. Hurrying to the hospital, I was shocked by what I saw. Richard was in intensive care and appeared very frail. He was heavily sedated and didn't seem to realize I was in the room. His condition deteriorated from there. Within two or three days his kidneys and liver had shut down, and he refused dialysis.

I guess in his mind it was time to go, but not in mine. I was having a really hard time adjusting, wrestling with what life would be like without my mentor and friend. We had just met. There was still so much more to learn. I wasn't ready to do what we had worked on without him.

Then, literally overnight, things changed—it was like someone realized Richard had too much unfinished business and revoked his departure. Walking into his room the next morning, I found Richard sitting up in bed asking where I'd been. I laughed in relief, telling him I had been there every day and asking where he had been. During the night his liver and kidneys had begun functioning, and it appeared he would recover. After a few weeks in the hospital he was back home and back to running his clothing business.

Every year on my birthday since the age of twenty, I have made a point of taking someone to dinner. During the month of September I ponder who has had the most profound impact on my life during the previous year. On the first of October that person receives an invitation to be my guest for a marvelous evening—my way of saying thank you. For my birthday in 1996 I had made up my mind long before September. I just needed my guest to be in good health and spirits.

Richard knew of my birthday tradition, and after he was well enough to go home, I gave him the invitation to join me for dinner at our restaurant, the Brown Stone. He was right when he said that writing my story for *Out Smart* magazine would change my life in ways I couldn't imagine. Richard was out of the hospital, in reasonably good health, and looking forward to the evening as much as I was.

My birthday in October 1996 was a day of pleasant surprises. I received a call from Shell's corporate director of diversity. She had received the SEA Shell survey from the CEO and wanted to meet the SEA Shell steering team for a discussion. Best damned birthday present I ever got.

By the end of September the survey document was available for SEA Shell members and management. Being on point as a signatory of the document, I was prepared and willing to field any questions. Initially, the only people who received copies of the survey report were those on the SEA Shell distribution. This was troublesome—I wanted the document to have broader circulation among the senior leadership of the company. During one of our conversations, I vented some of my frustration to Judy, who asked, "What do you want to do about it?" I replied, "I have half a mind to send copies of the survey report to my entire leadership chain all the way up to the CEO." Judy smiled and didn't have to ask the next question—I was out the door drafting letters and making copies of the survey to mail out.

Through the mailing event, a copy of the report had found its way to the corporate diversity director. She had had a meeting with the CEO, who shared his copy of the survey with her and asked that she follow up—thus the phone call on my birthday. About a week later a colleague and I were meeting with the diversity director. The meeting provided the opportunity to become acquainted and discuss topics of interest to a fledgling employee network—the big one being domestic partner benefits. Having come from a company with an established GLBT network, the diversity director was well versed on domestic partner benefits and the challenges for their implementation.

While domestic partner benefits were high on the list of SEA Shell objectives, the Shell leadership team was not well educated on the topic. Shell had created a benefits redesign team earlier in the year to review pension and health plans and offer recommendations on how they might be improved. As with the strategic team for diversity, the benefits redesign team was comprised of senior managers. They seemed to be following a similar approach of self-learning, benchmarking, and validating the recommendations that the strategic team for diversity had pursued.

There were opportunities to influence a decision on domestic partner benefits by the team. Focus groups were periodically assembled as a sounding board for the work of the benefits redesign team. While selection criteria for the focus group excluded any specific mention of sexual orientation, a few members of SEA Shell still made the cut. They may not have been out, but could still be voices in the room promoting more progressive policy changes, such as domestic partner benefits.

Judy had been an advocate with the benefits redesign team, soliciting information from me on domestic partner benefits, which she forwarded to team members. Upon finalizing the survey document, the SEA Shell steering committee also took the step of sharing the report with the benefits redesign team.

The diversity director's interest in SEA Shell's success seemed genuine. There was some hard work ahead, but where possible she offered resources and support. Much of the initial effort involved getting the network focused on refining its goals. She wanted to keep abreast of our progress by meeting monthly, and also expressed interest in potential opportunities for charitable outreach to the GLBT community.

Early outreach effort to the GLBT community had been tough. The first piece of outreach was in the fall of 1996. The Houston chapter of the group Parents, Families, and Friends of Lesbians and Gays (PFLAG) launched a billboard campaign along the freeways to raise awareness of the GLBT community, toward which the Westhollow Technologies Center made a contribution. The events that unfolded were also a learning experience. The company corporate contributions department rebuffed the opportunity, causing Westhollow to go it alone.

My speculation is that corporate contributions saw the opportunity as too risky and potentially attracting unwanted attention. Yet Westhollow made the contribution, the billboards went up, the press noted their existence, and I'm not aware of any backlash as a result. In fact, within the GLBT community, seeing

Shell listed as a sponsor turned some heads. People were pleasantly surprised by the interest Shell had shown in the project.

The diversity director also emphasized a need for SEA Shell to find allies among straight employees and managers in the company. I pondered who some of those people might be, based on my own interactions. The diversity director also passed along names of people in the business and HR she saw as supportive and felt would be approachable.

Ignorance of the issues was a formidable barrier to creating supporting equity for GLBT employees. When making inroads with leaders, my efforts were to understand where they were personally on GLBT workplace issues and how I could help further their grasp of the issues. Most leaders I approached seemed impressed by the quality of engagement and expressed a sincere interest in wanting to understand the issues. In most situations education helped—often I'd receive calls from managers recognizing they had GLBT employees in their department, wanting to be supportive, but not knowing how to demonstrate that support.

There were also some in management who felt their personal beliefs precluded them from being tolerant of a different sexual orientation. I found some quite polite and professional in their manner while promoting Shell as a company built on moral values and having no place for "perverse lifestyles." Others viewed diversity as just another program. If they could weather it long enough, this too would pass. This seemed to be a popular theme especially among colleagues who had been with the company long enough to experience other initiatives. Rather than waste limited time and resources, I often circumvented those who were unsupportive in search of straight allies with interest in SEA Shell and its mission.

When presented with requests from leaders to help with their learning about GLBT issues, I'd jump at the opportunities. One such opportunity with the HR organization occurred in early winter. HR chose to do a community service day in the Montrose and targeted some of the HIV/AIDS charities—a hospice and two service organizations. The day was an incredible learning experience for everyone, including myself. SEA Shell was invited to participate, and two of us did.

During the day I met and worked alongside a number of individuals involved in EEO/affirmative action, organizational development, benefits, medical, etc. When the work was done, we stopped at a local pub to debrief and socialize. The conversation was insightful—for many, this was their first exposure to people living with HIV/AIDS. Having a couple of SEA Shell members attend seemed to add to the learning. This was December 1996, and I found myself having to interject that while many believed only the GLBT community was affected by the virus, it was also spreading within straight society, and suburbia wasn't immune.

By year end 1996, everything was coming together. SEA Shell was on its feet and linked with the corporate diversity center. Domestic partner benefits, while still a long shot, were surviving and getting visibility in the benefits redesign efforts. Because of the survey, some of the business leaders were beginning to realize they had GLBT employees and wanted to understand their role in supporting appropriate workplace behaviors. I was also learning that for every action by SEA Shell there would be a need for a meaningful response. The seeds of an employee network were growing. How we as a network responded to various actions would define what we grew into.

Aligned with Richard's prediction, my life was changing in ways I couldn't have imagined. I was doing things I'd never realized I would do, like becoming a leader, learning to value people and their opinions, engaging executives, building trust, and fostering meaningful work relationships. Most importantly, I was learning—through books and the web, through people and experiences, and most importantly, through my mistakes.

Within a relatively short period of time Shell had changed their non-discrimination policy to include sexual orientation, I had my first gay publication, and a GLBT employee network was chartered. Outside the company I was exploring social and professional relationships with different organizations within the GLBT community. There was also a maturing of self. I was becoming more comfortable with who I was and the community with which I identified.

A lingering question for me was how to deploy SEA Shell for the betterment of the business. The short answer: Tie the network and the lessons to the values and business goals of the company. Over the coming years, details for achieving this alignment became more apparent. The network was engaging business leaders who wanted their organizations to be financially successful and obtain operational performance to make them leaders in the industry. So SEA Shell had to be able to answer two basic questions: 1) What was the business case for the network? and 2) How did this translate into a value proposition for the business and link to the core values of the company?

I didn't just wake up one day and decide to put together a successful employee network. There were lessons along the way, some of which were:

- Be open to new possibilities for your future and explore the elasticity of your imagination. Some things in life are hard to imagine, but they can happen if you embrace change.

- Developing and maintaining employee networks is hard work. Typically they're the result of a motivated few who have a genuine desire to create meaningful change for the better.

- Have a crisp business case and value proposition. A business wants to know what they're buying and the benefit (e.g. increased profitability, reputation and brand value with niche markets, employee morale/productivity, recruiting/retaining talent, etc.).

- Find an advisor or coach among senior management. He or she can be an effective mechanism for developing the GLBT network leadership team. The person doesn't have to be GLBT, just supportive and willing to learn.
- Develop a well-thought-out communication plan and build an effective partnership with the media relations organization.
- Outreach to the GLBT community may begin slowly—think about initial opportunities that allow a company to "test the waters." What they learn in the process helps them better understand the community and may encourage further outreach efforts.
- One cannot effectively lead from the closet. Companies need role models, real people in their organizations who are peers they relate to and work with.
- Change doesn't occur in a vacuum—it happens through established channels and systems in the company. A commitment to personal learning and quality engagement can open doors, providing opportunities to influence some of these systems and channels.
- Creating an employee network requires more voices than a half dozen people sitting in a room. Try to develop vehicles for bringing as many opinions and experiences as possible into the conversations. Some examples are surveys, focus groups, forums, etc.

One of my greatest struggles was balancing the demands of my full-time job with those of SEA Shell. For me personally the decision was easy; my first priority became creation of a safe, open workplace where everyone has the ability to achieve his or her full potential.

I knew there were possible repercussions in my performance rating as a result of placing an emphasis on diversity and GLBT workplace issues. But throughout life I've created a few rules for myself—one of which is, Sometimes the right answer isn't the easy answer, and at times it may not even be to your benefit, but it is still the right answer.

Fortunately, Judy and my supervisor understood the value proposition for creating a diverse, inclusive work environment and encouraged my further development in this area. In support of my efforts, a portion of my time was formally allocated for work in the area of diversity and became part of my performance contract.

Had my leaders not had the foresight to promote my development in this area, my life and career might well have taken a much different path. At times I've dwelt on the "what-ifs," but found the exercise to be counterproductive. I'd like to believe everything happens in life for a reason, and coming out when, where, and how I did was just part of a grander master plan.

5 Finding a Place at the Table

GLBT workplace issues weren't the only facet of diversity and inclusion gaining traction in the company. During the summer of 1996, the Westhollow Technologies Center leadership chartered a diversity council. Diversity councils are normally comprised of a cross-section of the organization, including representation from the business leadership. I responded to a solicitation for candidates interested in being part of the council and made the team. The diversity council worked with the leadership team in crafting a direction for diversity and inclusiveness at the site.

The team was very much a cross-section of the site, comprised of secretaries, technicians, engineers, scientists, and managers. Members were African-American, Asian, Hispanic, and Caucasian, male, female and of course, gay. To assure the team would be effective, three of the business directors participated on the team.

Aside from Judy and our secretary, I didn't know the other team members very well. Being diverse in composition didn't mean the team was also an enlightened group of people. We each had our own issues and behaviors to work through. I wrestled with how to put sexual orientation on the table along with everything else and in the process be attentive to my own blind spots around other differences. The best approach seemed to be a variation of what I had done up to this point—learn and teach. I would learn about issues of race, class, and gender from others in the room while helping them understand what life was like for gay employees.

I joined the team as an openly gay employee, expressing early on a desire to be a resource for their learning. The trick was putting enough information in the room to help people learn, yet not have sexual orientation dominate the team agenda. Striking the right balance was difficult at first—most of us had no formal training in the area of diversity and inclusion. By early fall the Westhollow diversity team had been scheduled for an awareness training session with the Westhollow Technologies Center leadership team and a few managers from other businesses, some of whom were my client base.

Heeding the advice of my peers, I had approached only a select few of my clients about my sexual orientation—most were fairly low on the corporate food chain. In contrast, some of the people in the room for the workshop were in positions that could very well affect the future of my career. Not knowing these leaders very well compounded my fears and hesitance to want to go forward.

My presence on the diversity team basically meant that sexual orientation was a given as part of the three-day offsite training, along with the topics of racism, sexism, and classism. Race and gender tend to be the core of most multi-subject diversity curricula. The piece on classism was added to increase awareness of the issues between the salaried and hourly staff, an evasive topic for a site with approximately 1,200 employees, about half of whom were hourly.

Up to this point I'd tried to be low-key about my sexual orientation, but the workshop was going to put me right out in front of everyone. I spent many nights unable to sleep, again staring at the ceiling, pondering whether coming out was such a good idea after all, beating myself up for listening to those people who had talked me into telling co-workers I was gay, thinking about how much easier life would have been if I had just stayed in the closet, wondering if this was going to destroy my career. What was I doing to myself?

Eventually my thoughts would drift to reflecting on life in the closet, the fear of being discovered or deprived of opportunities because of unwanted attention or scrutiny applied to my life, living two lives, having to lie and mislead others, trying to do my job well, but not too well. I knew being out wasn't going to be easy, but it was a burden I had chosen to bear. At least I was dealing with it on my own terms. Eventually Morpheus intervened and I was overcome by sleep.

Even though I had apprehensions about whether I had made the right decisions, I drew strength from Richard and Judy. There was a significant amount of preparation time involved on my part and theirs. They had been great coaches and mentors up to this point, and I grew to trust their judgment and have faith in their advice. Both knew the choices I was making were personally difficult. Judy briefed me on the content of the workshop and the people in the room—she would be there to support me if needed. Richard asked the tough questions about how I was feeling, what I was going to do in the workshop, where my safe harbor was, and how I would handle any backlash.

When the day of the workshop arrived, I was very nervous and afraid. There was nothing at that point that I could change shy of not showing up. I had not slept well, but I was too preoccupied with the coming events to care. More than anything I wanted to be comfortable and be myself. I put on jeans instead of slacks and one of my favorite shirts. There really was nothing I wanted to change about my appearance. I thought about taking out my earring, but that was a piece of me. I wasn't leaving parts of my identity behind just to be more appealing to people in the room.

I'd met the consultants, Marc and Shirley, prior to the workshop. They knew I was the "gay guy" in the room and were very supportive. The room arrangement was simple—a circle of chairs and some flip charts. There were about twenty-five participants, many of whom I didn't know. As I scanned the room I found Judy. Knowing where she was and being able to see her was reassuring.

The session started with introductions—participants were asked to share a little about themselves and what they hoped to get from the three days. Being near the end of the circle, I had more time than I really wanted to figure out what to say. While the introductions progressed, I agonized over whether this was the appropriate point to tell people about my sexual orientation. It was a mental exercise in plucking petals—I'll tell them, I won't, I'll tell them, I won't.

Finally it was my turn. After giving my name and talking about my job responsibilities, I dove off the cliff and talked about my sexual orientation. I consciously forced myself not to look at the floor or ceiling, but rather at the participants in the room.

Judy smiled as I spoke, which gave me the confidence to go on as I shared some of the anxiety I was feeling about being there that day. I also told them this wasn't about what I was feeling, but about their learning, which was more important to me than the fear I was suppressing. The body language around the room suggested that some were surprised, others were supportive, and some seemed indifferent. There was no opportunity for people to reply at this point. I would just have to see how they reacted to me during the rest of the workshop.

For the next three days we worked through issues of racial diversity, gender, class and heterosexism. Sexual orientation and heterosexism were tackled during the second day of the workshop. As part of the lesson we examined the stereotypes of the GLBT community and then broke into groups to develop workplace perceptions through the different lenses (i.e. white men, white women, people of color, and gay).

At this stage I was given a choice by the consultants: I could go with the group of white males and share my experiences as part of their group, or I could be a group of one and develop my own perceptions of the workplace as a gay man. I opted for the latter. Being part of the white male group would have been easier, but I felt my voice might not be heard when they summarized their conversations for the larger group. Thinking back on the information in the SEA Shell survey, I toiled away on my flip-charts, wanting to assure that more than just my views were present in the room.

The consultants brought everyone back together to share their output; I would be last. I was amazed at how little the other groups knew about gay society. Finally it was my turn to speak. I started by saying, "Being a group of one, I will try to be the voice for many." Launching forward, I talked about the derogatory jokes, fears of being fired or held back for promotion, domestic partner benefits issues, living two lives and more. I told them that personally, I'd rather focus my creative energy elsewhere, as it wasn't valued or appreciated in the workplace. So I focused on my community—working with the chamber and other organizations.

When I finally shut up, a long silence filled the room. I could feel my heart pounding, and the silence was becoming unnerving —a cough would have been welcome, anything but the silence. When it broke, the reaction that followed was one of denial and self-proclaimed ignorance of the issues. Yet for the first time in the workshop people seemed to be waking up, not just to the GLBT issues, but also to those for race, gender, and class.

Judy sat next to me during the group debrief. I was reassured when she whispered to me, "You don't have to reply to what people say—this isn't about you, it's about them." Some voiced their comfort with the stereotypes for the GLBT community, but saw me differently and struggled with the paradox. Others expressed a desire to learn more.

Then there was that one person in the room who just didn't get it—saying he didn't discriminate, yet associating homosexuality, pedophilia, and bestiality as though they were synonymous. The comment went unaddressed because I think no one, including myself, really knew what to do with it in the grander scheme of things. The statement mortified me, and feeling a sense of intimidation from my surroundings, I couldn't even begin to think of how to compose a response.

For some there is the perception that all gay people are pedophiles, while studies show most pedophiles are actually heterosexuals. The perception drives the stereotype, even though facts are to the contrary. But because of the perception, I often find myself shying away from children. On one occasion at a mall, I went to use one of the public restrooms. Outside was a woman waiting for her son, who had apparently been in the restroom for a while. She asked if I would check on him and bring him out to her. I respectfully declined. I wasn't about to go check on somebody's kid in a men's restroom. On the way out I saw the boy playing with the faucets on the sinks and relayed the news to his mother, but I wasn't going to bring him out to her.

As for the reference to bestiality, I can only surmise that in the context of the statement the person was grouping sexual behaviors other than heterosexual intercourse to make a point. I inferred the meaning to be that based on limited information and prevalent stereotypes, in the mind of this individual, bestiality, homosexuality, and pedophilia were synonymous. But I wasn't in a position to debate or lecture the point. I was trying to bounce back from the shock of the statement.

As the workshop drew to a close I found myself mentally drained—we all were. I was feeling very vulnerable. I quietly made my way to the door, but not before being confronted by a number of the leaders in the room wanting to voice their recognition of the courage it had taken for me to step out and help in their education. Several of those leaders stayed in touch after the workshop, utilizing me as a resource to help in their continued development in demonstrating support for GLBT employees in the workplace.

As tough as the three days had been on me, they also helped me grow. Courage was the farthest thing from my mind entering the room—the more appropriate word for me was "survival." Going into the session, I was concerned about the impact on my career and salvaging what I could afterward. Being a resource to others continuing their learning was not a personal expectation coming out of the room. I had grown; my confidence in myself was not only intact, but reinforced by the experience. I could do this work.

During the diversity workshop I had a chance to speak with a couple of members of the benefits redesign team about how domestic partnership benefits were faring. One of them shared that in the grand scheme of things, domestic partner benefits were such a little piece of the pie compared to pension and health that they probably wouldn't make the package. WRONG ANSWER! I relayed back to the SEA Shell members on the focus group the importance of keeping the topic on the table, which they were able to achieve.

After the workshop the Westhollow Diversity Council was basically established. As I surveyed the people on the team, it was difficult to determine where they were on the topic of sexual orientation. There were several who subscribed to strong Christian values, among them the person who referred to homosexuality, bestiality and pedophilia in the workshop as though they were synonymous. Still, I knew some were supportive based on their behavior in the workshop. My challenge was to further my own understanding of differences and become a credible resource to the team on issues pertaining to GLBT employees.

After the workshop, core groups were formed, each comprised of three or four participants from the workshop. The core groups were visibly diverse, voluntary, self-structured, and focused on furthering participants' education after the workshop.

Each made its own decisions about how often to meet and on topics for further learning. As with any voluntary effort, some groups thrived while others withered.

I was fortunate to be in one of the groups that thrived. The other participants in my core group were a white male from the health and safety organization, an African-American woman who was also a single parent, and an older white male who was the HR director for the technologies center. All of us had a reason for wanting to promote diversity. For me it was about creating a safe, open workplace where everyone had the opportunity to achieve his or her potential. Others wanted to right some of the systemic injustices of the past, promote equity and have an impact on the world they wanted their kids to grow up in. Some saw the world changing, and when they sat at a traffic light and looked around at other cars, they saw people who looked different from them. If the company were to thrive in this world, it would have to embrace those different people.

Our first few meetings were on site in a conference room, where we talked about our backgrounds and potential learning opportunities. I had suggested that for a future meeting we take a lunch field trip to the Montrose. Everyone was game, so we set it up, and the next meeting was at Baba Yega, an old cottage in the heart of the Montrose that had been turned into a café.

It was a fantastic learning venue. We talked about impressions of the Montrose, the gay community, and our surroundings. Had I not told them that many of the patrons were gay, they would not have been able to discern a difference. One cannot distinguish another person's sexual orientation simply by looking at him or her. We were surrounded by business people having lunch; some were straight, some happened to be gay, and some were transgender.

Just a few yards away was the bar district. Down on Westhiemer were other eateries and shops, some of which were gay-owned. The group members discussed the difference between the restaurant crowd and the GLBT stereotypes. I shared with them that the bar scene in the evening was a bit different, but basically a microcosm of society in general. The field trip was stimulating to our learning as well as our taste buds. So we did other events exploring Asian cuisine, kosher foods, and soul food.

Not all that we experienced was at the lunch table. Richard had suggested that I arrange an after work field trip that took our group to AIDS Foundation Houston. It was an astounding experience even for me. The director of AIDS Foundation Houston gave each of us a small bag of different colored M&M's. The candy was a simulation of medications a person with HIV/AIDS might be taking. With the bag came instructions on how each different colored M&M was to be preserved (room temperature or refrigerated) and how often they were to be taken. The exercise was to take the candy home and try to adhere to the instructions for taking the "medication"—for me getting up in the middle of the night was tough, not to mention no fridge in my office at work where I could keep those that required refrigeration.

The stigma society attaches to HIV/AIDS forces many to want to keep their diagnosis and treatment confidential. Think about the justifications someone would have to go through to get a refrigerator in his or her office. What would it be like for a person who is not gay, but HIV positive? What are the perceptions others would have of the person?

I also had a whole different understanding of what life was like for Richard and some of my other friends who were HIV-positive or struggling with AIDS. Some had not yet reached the stage of needing medication, while the hopes of others relied on trials for different protease inhibitors. While the exercise provided an insight into the rigors associated with taking the medications, it couldn't illuminate the side effects of some of the medications.

I really marveled at Richard. He was active on the boards of several community organizations, ran his own clothing business, battled an illness ravaging his body, and still found time to mentor and coach me and others. How he found the time and strength to remain so active was truly remarkable. Yet in his mind he didn't know how much time was left, and he was going to use every minute of what he had to help others.

One of the most effective features of the Diversity Council was the direct linkage established to the leadership team for the technologies center. The leaders were intimately involved in the planning, providing a litmus test for recommendations on how to implement diversity initiatives at the site. As the Diversity Council developed a charter and plan for integrating diversity at the technologies center, I periodically interjected information about issues pertaining to sexual orientation—first my coming out story, then the SEA Shell survey results, and some key references from websites and books.

Some of the material dwelled on personal experiences of other employees in the company and what life was like for them in the workplace. There were stories of people not out at work hearing the disparaging jokes and comments about gay people from coworkers, and others taking vacation time to care for a sick partner. Other materials offered suggestions on how managers and employees could show support for GLBT employees even if none were out in their workplace.

Just because a business has a diversity council doesn't mean ready acceptance of training on the topic of sexual orientation. While the Westhollow technologies center was making progress, the IT business was struggling with sexual orientation in their learning process. Though various meetings had occurred on the topic and leaders in IT had met with members of SEA Shell, their diversity council decided not to work the topic of sexual orientation in their initial training plans.

For me the training on the topic of sexual orientation in the workplace was important for a couple of reasons: 1) The non-discrimination policy had been changed, a GLBT network was in place, and domestic partner benefits were likely to follow. 2) Managers seemed to be struggling with the subject matter and with differentiating between expected behaviors in the workplace and individual beliefs.

My underlying premise was that treating everyone with dignity and respect should be an expected behavior. The message I tried to portray to others was that employees were a valuable resource and they should be developed and leveraged. Individual beliefs were not grounds for justifying prejudice. Treating people with dignity and respect was consistent with the Shell core value, "belief in people." While the wording of the values and business principles has evolved over the years, the meaning remains.

With diversity councils forming and a corporate diversity director on board, visible change was creeping into the organizational culture of Shell. Judy had expressed interest in the corporate diversity director position, but the decision was made early on to hire from the outside. The new director was beginning to gather the threads of diversity and inclusion already spun before her arrival and weaving them into the fabric of a corporate diversity strategy.

While sporadic, the topic of sexual orientation was beginning to receive airtime in some of the businesses. Over several months the Westhollow Diversity Council found its course and set off on creating a better workplace. With the help of an external diversity consultant, the Diversity Council developed a strategy and could plan forward. Training was a piece of the picture—beginning with the managers. The Diversity Council and the Westhollow leadership agreed the training would cover the topics of race, gender, class, and sexual orientation.

In response to adding the module on sexual orientation, I committed to having at least one or two SEA Shell members in each of the workshops. During the module, people would break into groups and go through exercises designed to dissect the stereotype for sexual orientation. Having openly gay people in the room during the workshop gave a face and real presence to the topic.

I made the commitment of having one or two SEA Shell members in each workshop, not knowing if I would be able to deliver. The workshop I experienced had helped me grow, and I felt others wanting to explore being out in the workplace should have the same opportunity. When I shared the opportunity with SEA Shell, describing the experience and asking if others were willing to go through sessions, the response was very favorable. Getting enough people was not a problem.

Having gone through the workshop experience alone, I knew how draining it could be. So on the second night of each workshop, when the class finished the sexual orientation piece, as it let out I would meet the SEA Shell members, go have a beer and listen and learn about their experiences. I did this out of a genuine personal desire to be sure they were all right.

For many, this was their first taste of stepping out of the closet and testing the water. There were adrenaline rushes, anxieties, and for most, I think, a sense of self-confidence. Most of the SEA Shell participants in the workshops eventually came out at work. I don't know how profound an impact the workshop experiences had in their decisions, but I'd like to think they helped. With the training and strategic plan in place, diversity was off and running at Westhollow.

However, this was not without some pain and consternation. A member of the diversity council continued to see sexual orientation as a personal, private "lifestyle" that should not be invoked or condoned in the workplace. The situation finally came to a head—during a joint meeting of the Westhollow leadership team and the Diversity Council, the individual once again compared homosexuality, bestiality, and pedophilia. Once again, with the patience of a saint, I let it slide, even though I found the statements troubling and discomforting.

For one of my straight team members, however, this was the final straw that broke the camel's back. Eva, a member of the team who worked in HR, confronted the other individual on the remarks. To my surprise, and everyone else's in the room, Eva stopped our meeting and undertook the task of working through how to prevent these disparaging remarks from reoccurring. Rather than constructively work through the issue, the individual who had been making the remarks chose to leave the meeting.

All I could think about was how this was my fault, and if I hadn't been on the team, this never would have happened. After the person walked out of the meeting, there was an eerie silence in the room. All eyes seemed focused on me, what I was feeling, and how people could help. I was very proud of Eva and will be forever grateful for what she did for me that day. I was also very proud of my other team members and the leadership team, who stood firmly with me and were supportive. It was at that point that I realized these were people who genuinely cared about creating a better workplace for everyone. Later, in a very terse note the individual resigned from the Diversity Council, stating that validation of a homosexual "lifestyle" was a violation of his religious freedom.

Here's my thing on religion: in the workplace there are expected behaviors—among them, people should be treated with dignity and respect. I do not condone someone being disrespectful or showing prejudice toward a person with strong religious values, and I will not condone someone using their religious values to be disrespectful or prejudicial toward someone of a different gender identity or sexual orientation.

Training was just the beginning—the Diversity Council became aware of the "Safe Listeners" program created by AT&T and wanted to explore something similar for the Westhollow Technology Center. Benchmarking the efforts of AT&T, the Diversity Council explored a similar program, but expanded the concept.

Using a green tree for the logo, the Westhollow program was structured to include all differences.

The "Safe Listeners" program required training and adherence to specific guidelines. The program would not circumvent existing HR policies and procedures, just identify safe space for an employee to talk with someone else about what the workplace was like for him or her. If the employee felt harassed or had a complaint, the safe listener would encourage the person to take the issue to management and/or HR. Not everyone was suited to be a safe listener, and HR took an active role in the program, supporting and nurturing the concept.

All my commitments to diversity and SEA Shell were chiseling time away from my real job and filling my schedule outside of work. I had negotiated a portion of my time be dedicated to diversity-related topics, and had diversity goals as well as technical goals. I used a diversity charge code for up to 15% of my time. Anything over 15% was my own personal time—a tangible indicator of the priority this work had in my life.

With the changes occurring in Shell came varying responses, some good, some not so good. After changing the non-discrimination policy, I had the opportunity to read a letter sent to the CEO. The author charged that by promoting sexual orientation as part of diversity, we were making Shell a haven for people with perverted sexual preferences. The hatred infused in the words of those pages made me tremble with anger. How dare someone suggest I be governed under his or her beliefs and ignorance! What gave this person the right to judge me because of my sexual orientation? How dare the letter writer call it a "preference" and suggest I'm perverted because of the way I came into this world?

I cried. I shut the door to my office and cried. Someone in the company hated me because I was gay. We'd never met, he knew nothing about my performance, yet because of my sexual orientation, judgment was passed—I must be a bad person. Later the same day I caught a plane to North Carolina. I tucked a copy of the letter in my backpack before I headed for the airport.

While on the flight I was determined to find some good in the letter and began reading it over and over. After about a dozen reviews, I found the good. By then there was no more pain, no more anger, no more tears. The letter had become words on pages and nothing more. I could rise above it.

I realized this was just the beginning of what I'd be exposed to. As the diversity initiatives progressed, there would be push back. For some, the initiatives would be greeted as providing opportunities, yet others would see mostly risks to their careers. From my experiences thus far, several points were becoming quite clear:

- Just because a company had a diversity council didn't mean the council was on board with all facets of difference. I had blind spots about other people's differences, and others had some for GLBT workplace issues. Learning together assured everyone a place at the table.
- Straight allies were important to gaining traction on GLBT workplace issues. As they became more comfortable with the subject matter, they tended to be more supportive of a broader agenda for inclusion.
- I had to pick my battles, taking on those challenges offering the most opportunity for advancing the cause of equity. If straight allies wanted to take on a few of those battles, I welcomed the company.
- Learning to temper my reactions and maintain composure was going to be critical if I was to be an effective role model for GLBT workplace issues going forward.
- I have feelings just like everyone else. Repeatedly reading the letter sent to the CEO forced me to block those feelings and apply my intellect to bring reason into the equa-

> tion. I was training myself to suppress my emotions to become a tougher, more rational force when confronted with indignities.

I know there are people in this world that hate me and wish me harm simply because of my sexual orientation. I also know I didn't "choose" my sexual orientation any more so than heterosexuals do. Yet these people do not govern my life, nor am I as an individual in any way compelled to adhere to their sense of reality or artificial norms. If the road ahead was to be rocky, then I was up to the task.

6 The Push for Domestic Partner Benefits

I believe people enter and exit our lives for a reason. While it might not be readily apparent upon meeting, we have something to share with each other. The trick is making the most of the relationship in order to garner the learning. If one takes all these relationships seriously, a mosaic forms with the potential to influence and shape our thinking and behaviors.

Throughout much of my adult life I've been developing a mosaic of people, primarily out of a genuine interest—one of my personal core values. I believe this core affinity for people drives my interest and passion for helping others. It all seems to tie back to leaving home for college at the age of nineteen. My family life was in complete disarray, my parents in the beginnings of a protracted and messy divorce fueled by greed, mistrust, and selfishness.

When I arrived at university, I knew absolutely no one. With the domestic chaos at home, I was feeling very much alone in the world and needed a surrogate home environment, not something most people are willing to offer. I learned hard lessons about making friends. I also learned more than I had expected to about myself—some good and some not so good. The challenges were made more formidable as I wrestled with my sexual orientation.

For the first time in my life I was acutely aware of the importance of relationships and earning trust. I've long retained interest in people, meeting many along the way, some of whom have been close friends for decades, and others the surrogate family I longed to find. Listening and learning about others makes me pause to re-examine the man I've been growing up to be—my strengths and weaknesses and how they manifest in me as a person.

The challenge has always been about overcoming my shyness in order to meet someone and understanding the work required to maintain friendships. It's difficult for me to just walk up to someone and strike up a conversation. I need a context for the dialogue, a beginning—analogous to asking someone to dance.

In fact, maintaining a relationship is much like dancing, requiring effort on the part of both parties to make it work. The effort each invests contributes to the natural longevity and quality of the friendship. At different times one or the other leads, often necessitated by a desire to move together to a different place. Ultimately both people gain from a common sense of choreography.

How does all this fit into the workplace? When the diversity director recommended finding straight allies in the workplace, she gave license to network, a context for meeting senior leaders, and the ability to develop meaningful relationships. She provided a venue for influencing change at various levels of the organization.

The ability to engage leaders and effectively influence change and build support from straight allies required the efforts of more than three openly gay people in the company. SEA Shell's greatest strength has always been its membership, both in numbers and positions in the business. They continue to be among the best and the brightest, representing a vast amount of intellectual property. But more people had to be influenced to come out and support the work of creating an inclusive work environment.

To help orchestrate mobilizing the membership, the diversity director assisted in a variety of ways—providing the finances to bring in a consultant to work with SEA Shell to finalize the group's charter, facilitating SEA Shell interaction with the most senior business leaders, supporting the adoption of domestic partner benefits, and strategically intervening in the growth of SEA Shell's membership. We still had to do the work and make it happen, but her support and efforts were most welcome.

During the first quarter of 1997, when leaders in the oil products business were talking about diversity and Judy was in the room, SEA Shell had an ally and sexual orientation was on the agenda. One day when I dropped by Judy's office for one of our regular updates, she shared that the vice president of marketing and his leadership were interested in spending a day working on the topic of sexual orientation. To make the experience effective, marketing wanted a couple of gay employees in the room. Having grown up in the marketing organization, I really wanted to be one of the people, and Judy concurred. I shot a note off to SEA Shell to see if anyone else wanted to take part—one of my out colleagues replied back and we both attended.

There was another driver for doing these workshops. The benefits redesign team was preparing to do a cross-business briefing on their work. Up to this point SEA Shell had been able to keep domestic partner benefits on the table, but it wasn't clear how they would fare in the cross-business meeting. Having as many informed leaders as possible in the room was crucial.

Walking into the workshop, I already knew several of the players. In the marketing organization, these were the people with a reputation of making or breaking careers. The vice president was a very domineering figure. Knowing how much power and authority they had, I struggled not to be intimidated by their presence. The consultants helped by establishing some basic ground rules for how the workshop would be conducted. This was my second workshop, the first (about two months prior) having been the one for the Westhollow Leadership and Diversity Council. Fortunately, the consultants were Marc and Shirley, who had facilitated the first workshop at Westhollow. It was a relief having a couple of friendly faces in the room.

The consultants began the session by having us pair up with someone in the room we didn't know very well to share who we were and what we wanted to get out of the day. Before I could pair up, I heard someone calling my name. It was the marketing vice president—he knew everyone in the room reasonably well, so it made sense for us to pair up, but that didn't make it easy.

The vice president started by telling me how his father had been a painter. He had known a number of gay people while growing up. He wanted to gain a better understanding of the workplace issues for GLBT employees. After he finished, I shared my purpose of wanting to help with his learning, becoming a resource to him and his team.

After the exchange with the marketing vice president, something occurred to me—I had just had a conversation with "the person" rather than the vice president. This was a key realization —up to this point I had allowed myself to be intimidated by titles, which were really only a façade.

As the day unfolded, the conversations began with defining a common vocabulary. The open discussions throughout the day touched on religious issues, personal values, same-gender families raising children, and domestic partner benefits.

The discussions on values and religion were often intertwined. I reminded them that one of Shell's core values was "belief in people." How did they interpret this core value? Another core value was trust. How could one build trust with co-workers if they couldn't bring their whole selves to work? Being openly gay in the workplace had nothing to do with challenging anyone's religious beliefs—it had everything to do with my being able to live up to the core values and expectations of the company. Regardless of religious values or sexual orientation, I was expected to perform to the best of my ability to help the company achieve its business goals. If I had to expend energy to physically and mentally manage hiding a part of my identity, then that was effort wasted and was inhibiting my productivity.

I digressed to talk about what it was like for me back in the early 1990s while working in the marketing organization. I had shied away from conversations about my social life and was evasive about whom I was dating. My intuition told me the workplace would not be accepting of someone who was gay, so I hid that part of my identity from my co-workers. These actions didn't exactly build trust and meaningful work relationships with my colleagues. Sure, I did my work, but I wasn't as productive as I could have been.

Retelling some of my stories of what life in the marketing organization had been like while I was still in the closet was very beneficial. The trip with colleagues through the streets of San Francisco shortly after I started, my roommate that pulled a knife and my having to move without people in the office knowing, the response of people in my work group about the Jeffery Collins lawsuit, had all happened while I was working in the marketing organization.

If they didn't think there was a business case for being sensitive to issues of homophobia or heterosexism, I gave them one. While assigned to the West Coast, I had heard an engineer airing his frustration with progress on environmental remediation of a service station in San Francisco. He was irritated with the "faggot" living nearby who stirred up the neighborhood, resulting in budget overruns on the cleanup of the site. Others told me the engineer chose to ignore the neighbor when he called to inquire about the activities at the service station. As the story goes, he perceived the neighbor to be gay and seemed to be ignoring him for that reason. If this was really the case, a homophobic response had led to the involvement of someone on city council, community meetings, other consultants being hired, and more testing being done to reassure the public—not a cheap proposition.

The general feedback from the marketing leaders at the end of the workshop was good. It's hard for me to get a sense of what those in the room really took away. The consultants thought it a productive and successful day. About a month later I had a better understanding of the impact from the workshop.

The leadership of the Shell businesses and firms gathered at the Woodlands resort north of the city for a conference on the benefits redesign efforts. The feedback I received from people present during the meetings was that most attendees were in favor of the benefits redesign package, including the proposal on domestic partner benefits. There were a couple of managers in each of the businesses that voiced objections to the provision, but the majority were either silent or vocally in support. Among those vocally in support were some of the marketing managers who had gone through the workshop on sexual orientation just a few weeks prior.

This wasn't the end of the road for the benefits redesign. They still had to be blessed by the U.S. leadership team and approved by the board for Shell Oil Company. After the conference, I was told the recommendation for domestic partner benefits was for further study, which I equated to mean there was still opposition. SEA Shell still had work to do if they wanted the benefits.

SEA Shell members in the IT business had wanted a meeting with their division president and his management team for a while. Since he was a member of the Shell U.S. leadership team, the diversity director had suggested waiting until after SEA Shell had formalized its mission and goals, which was set to happen in early March of 1997.

Opposition to domestic partner benefits was more visible after the Woodland conference. Some wrote personal notes to their managers and members of the benefits redesign team. The following excerpt gives an idea of the arguments posed:

> *From personal experience, I have found that anything not founded on the Word of God is not going to last long. About a year and a half ago I began to pray two things for Shell. First, I pray that Shell leadership will be Christians who seek God for direction when es-*

tablishing policy and making decisions. Second, I pray that the values the company adopts are Biblical values. I too want my company to be the Premier Company and believe firmly that one of the keys is to operate according to these Biblical values. I applaud our Core Values because I think they conform to these values. Unfortunately, providing benefits to domestic partners, whose sole qualification for the benefits is fornication with the employee, does not follow Biblical values.

Some leaders who received mail like this had encouraged the authors to talk to me about their views—they never did. I don't think the conversations would have been very productive. I would have emphasized the core values of the company and the expected behaviors in the workplace, which probably wouldn't have resonated very well. The lack of interest on the part of the authors to have a meaningful discussion suggested to me they were set in their opinions and had no interest in hearing the other side of the story. What I found more intriguing was the assumption by the author that everyone on the distribution for the correspondence was straight, or had no gay friends or family. I guess it never occurred to some that gay people might have the same faith-based values and beliefs as others, and find solace in the study of the Bible.

Like many other companies, Shell had a large network of Bible study groups that usually gathered during the lunch hour. While typically limited to discussions of scripture, one note went a bit further by adding:

There will be a letter stating basic beliefs of those who are against Shell putting into effect policies that deal with granting benefits to "domestic partners." Our statement will be in the form of a petition letter allowing all those who would like to sign to do so. We would like to get as many of you who are convicted on this issue to sign, but in the same respect, we do not want to bother those who are not concerned. If you do not want to be approached with this letter, please just reply back to this note with a quick "not interested" and your response will be honored.

A friend, Margaret, thought it prudent I be made aware of what was "stirring in the grass" and forwarded the note. Margaret shared that she and others in the Bible study group had responded back as not interested. That reaffirmed my faith in Christianity. Many of the names on the distribution for the Bible study group were familiar to me—they were good people.

Still, I couldn't begin to find the words to express the irritation and hurt I felt when reading the note from the Bible study group. From a spiritually-based perspective, they probably thought domestic partner benefits undermined the values they saw as governing the company. From my point of view, they were invoking their will on making my life and the lives of others more difficult. After all, someone had taken time out of their busy workday to assemble this epistle because they felt obliged to intervene on something that had no direct impact on them.

SEA Shell had gone through the hurdles of defining how it would constructively use the Shell e-mail system to promote diversity and inclusion, seeking permission from the company to do so. Yet some in the Bible study groups seemed quite comfortable using the system in a manner that seemed contrary to this end.

What I was wrestling with was the perceived personal attack. The people in the Bible study group weren't attacking me; they were attacking the adding of domestic partner benefits, which they saw as undermining their value system. Yet the benefits were important to others in the GLBT workforce and to me. So I felt a sense of ownership and took the petition as a personal affront.

Later in the day I stopped by to see Richard and told him about the petition. His reply was not to try to fight every battle, and if you must fight, to do so honorably—don't stoop to their level. I heard his words, and with every last ounce of composure, I continued to treat all with dignity and respect. I maintained my integrity and remained professional. I was getting very good at handling the pain and leaving the tears at home. I tried to focus my anger constructively, using the energy to help SEA Shell thrive.

A key milestone for SEA Shell was becoming formally chartered. The steering team wanted as many members of SEA Shell as possible to attend an offsite meeting. Most of SEA Shell's members were not out at work. They were torn between wanting to participate in the creation of the network and having to explain their absence to their supervisors without divulging their sexual orientation.

In response, the Corporate Diversity Center provided a letter for employees to give to their supervisors stating that the employee was selected for a focus group to support development of future diversity initiatives for the company. The letter was for those SEA Shell members wanting to attend the meeting, but needing something in writing to give to their supervisor. Even with the letter, the supervisor still had the ability to deny the request.

About twenty SEA Shell members attended the offsite meeting held at the Lovett Inn. Wanting to support the GLBT community, I checked with the Greater Houston GLBT Chamber of Commerce to research hotels that were members. At the time only the Lovett Inn was a member, so that was my recommendation to the SEA Shell steering committee, which they supported. The SEA Shell workshop was a first for Shell in supporting a GLBT community business. The Lovett Inn was glad to have us, and the price for the two days was quite competitive with other hotels in the area. Some members coming into town from Louisiana actually stayed at the inn. Over the years SEA Shell continued to use the Lovett Inn for other events until eventually outgrowing the space.

The diversity director had arranged a meeting between the consultant facilitating the SEA Shell workshop and some of the Shell U.S. leadership team the day before our workshop. For many of the leaders, this was their first formal introduction to the topic of sexual orientation in the workplace. The primary focus of the discussion was the importance of treating people equitably in the workplace and the business case for domestic partner benefits.

The president of the IT business was among those in the room. He expressed a lack of understanding on GLBT workplace issues and a willingness to meet with SEA Shell to learn more. That meeting set the stage for a dinner between SEA Shell and the president of the IT business. The event presented the first opportunity for SEA Shell members to meet with a leader of one of the Shell businesses.

The diversity director kicked off the opening of the two-day SEA Shell workshop. She emphasized the importance of networking, encouraging people to come out, and making SEA Shell a viable resource for the company. Having her there for the opening sent a clear message that GLBT workplace issues were a part of diversity and she was genuinely interested in creating an environment of inclusion. By the end of the first day, SEA Shell had hammered out the mission statement:

> The mission of SEA Shell is to provide support for members and co-workers, promote equality for employees regardless of sexual orientation, and create awareness in management of issues and concerns affecting people in a diverse workplace.

The group had also narrowed its original long list of goals to the following four after removing redundancies and building on common themes:

- SEA Shell will support education and awareness of Shell's staff and management on current issues concerning sexual orientation in the workplace. This will include participation in curriculum development and delivery, as well as providing resources to support diversity education in this area.
- SEA Shell will work with management to ensure the rapid and effective implementation of domestic partner benefits.

- SEA Shell will provide an opportunity for its members to network within Shell and with similar employee groups in other corporations. We will further explore opportunities for Shell to demonstrate its commitment to its gay and lesbian employees and to the community at large in a manner that is consistent with Shell's core values.
- We will encourage and support Shell's health services organization to develop HIV/AIDS and other STD education to the benefit of all Shell employees.

These goals clearly supported the mission statement, providing an overarching context within which the governance structure could effectively operate. Sub-committees were formed around education, domestic partner benefits, and outreach to support the work. The fourth goal was to be worked on directly with the Shell health services organization, giving them ownership.

A portion of time was also allocated to talk about the upcoming meeting with the president of the IT business. The basic question on the table was whether we wanted a meeting with the "president" or the "person." Most agreed it was the person—leaders need to be on a personal learning journey. While focusing on what's best for the company, they also have to consider the influence their own value system has on corporate decision-making.

If I'm not personally comfortable with a subject, the decision-making process tends to be more difficult. The easy response to these situations is to want to reject or dismiss the issue and move on with more important business at hand. As a leader I realized there was a responsibility to keep learning if I was going to be effective at making informed decisions for which I would be accountable.

SEA Shell had to give some thought to what they wanted to take away from the meeting with the IT president and what they wanted to leave with him and his entourage in the way of information. The big issues for SEA Shell were domestic partner benefits, assurance that policies would be visibly communicated to all employees, and the creation of a safe, supportive work environment for GLBT employees wanting to come out.

SEA Shell members also came up with some thoughts about how to structure the meeting with the IT president. The meeting would be over dinner at an offsite location. The basic questions to be answered: Who would be attending from SEA Shell? What would be the ground rules for the meeting? What were the expectations of SEA Shell and of the IT president? What were the perceptions of the IT organization for GLBT employees?

Originally, the plan was to have any SEA Shell members willing to volunteer, as only a few were out at work. With a little coaching and refining of some ground rules, several SEA Shell members from the IT organization who were not out expressed interest in the event. This was a fortuitous decision—having gay people from the business meet with the leaders and share their stories about life in the IT organization was very powerful.

Ground rules were important. They created the "safe container" for people to be themselves, talk and learn. The trick was hammering out a set of rules that didn't restrain the learning or leave either party at a disadvantage in the conversation. The one thing important to SEA Shell members who would be out in the room was that the leaders not out them later in the workplace. The meeting wasn't going to be about making demands. SEA Shell was going into the room to share, listen and learn—they wanted the same from the IT leaders.

About a week after the SEA Shell workshop, I had a monthly meeting with the diversity director to frame up our next steps for the dinner meeting with the IT president. Prior to the dinner meeting, she wanted to know who was going, meet with them, and understand the structure of the conversation. She asked that I forward the president of the IT business a copy of the SEA Shell survey and follow up with a call to get a feel for his expectations for the evening.

With the next steps outlined for the meeting, we switched to another topic, domestic partner benefits. The diversity director inquired if SEA Shell members would be willing to send notes of support to the CEO. Many people had been sending notes opposing the benefits, but none had sent any in support. It wouldn't hurt to ask.

I short-listed the total number of SEA Shell members attending the dinner meeting to seven, including Judy and myself. During the pre-meeting with the diversity director, we clearly laid out the agenda for the meeting and who would say what. I had contacted the president of the IT business, who shared with me his interest in learning about the issues, emphasizing that he wanted it to be a comfortable event for everyone attending. SEA Shell attendees would each take a topic: the importance of being out at work, domestic partner benefits, reasons for awareness training, and the impact of changing the Shell nondiscrimination policy to include sexual orientation.

SEA Shell also gave thought to what they needed out of the meeting, which was a mechanism for future dialogue with the IT president and his managers. We needed to know whether he would approach other business leaders about participating in awareness sessions on sexual orientation and raise with HR the review and revision of policies to make sure they were aligned with the wording change of the non-discrimination policy.

The night of the dinner, SEA Shell members were the first to arrive. Shortly thereafter the IT president, his entourage, and the diversity director entered the room. The expressions on some of their faces were priceless. I had found out prior that some of the SEA Shell members attending were highly regarded by some of these leaders for their job performance. Yet the leaders had no idea these employees were gay until they walked into the room. You can't tell someone's sexual orientation simply by appearance or mannerisms.

The IT president started out by confirming that this was a chance for him and his leaders to learn about workplace issues and understand what the work environment was like for their GLBT employees. As the meeting began, members of SEA Shell each took a topic and put it on the table. They kept opening remarks on each of their topics to a few minutes. Then everyone had a chance to ask questions and build on the dialogue.

There was a genuine interest on the part of the IT leadership to understand why people felt so passionate about being out in the workplace and the relevance of domestic partner benefits. Education felt like a tougher sell. By the end of the meeting SEA Shell had put forth ideas they hoped the IT president and his staff would consider taking forward. The IT president was willing to consider awareness sessions for senior leaders, and SEA Shell offered support if needed. We also offered to help answer questions or provide additional information on domestic partner benefits. There were no commitments and none expected—just our offer of help to support their learning and development.

Afterward I offered to buy drinks for the SEA Shell attendees at Baba Yega, a local Houston restaurant and bar in the heart of the Montrose district. Several took me up on the offer as a chance to debrief. As we walked up the sidewalk, I could see Judy and the IT leadership ahead of us. She had participated in the meeting in the role of a senior management advisor to SEA Shell. While not officially a role at the time, I felt her presence in the room had helped validate SEA Shell as a resource. She was hammering away on them about something. I don't know what she said, but I was very grateful she was on our side.

At Baba Yega, everyone was just coming down off the adrenaline rush. Many shared that the experience was incredible—they had all done such a terrific job, very articulate, credible, professional. I was very proud of every one of them. Most had never been out in the workplace, and now the door was cracked open. One woman was so excited with how events had played out that her immediate response was, "What's next!"

The leadership of the IT business left a good impression on SEA Shell attendees. The members were also very impressed with Judy. Not really knowing her that well, they were amazed that a straight ally would be so openly supportive of their cause in front of other leaders. Whether IT business leaders carried through on SEA Shell's requests or not, SEA Shell attendees respected them for making time and genuinely listening.

Prior to the dinner, I had also sent an e-mail to all SEA Shell members informing them that the CEO would be interested in hearing from them should they want to write in support of domestic partner benefits. I asked in their notes that they consider why it was important to them. I also sent notes out to the Westhollow Technologies Center Diversity Council and others I knew to be supportive of the cause, asking them to write. During a debrief after the dinner with the IT president, the diversity director told me the CEO was overwhelmed by the responses supporting the benefits.

Shell wasn't the only oil company struggling to obtain domestic partner benefits. Chevron (now ChevronTexaco) was also heading down that road. Chevron had been one of the first oil companies to add sexual orientation to their non-discrimination policy and create an employee network group. I had shared this insight with the Shell benefits redesign team. Announcing domestic partner benefits before Chevron would have given Shell a lead over the competition in the energy industry on GLBT workplace issues. I really wanted Shell to start leading on some of these issues. I was tired of being behind the curve.

By late spring the benefits redesign package had run the full course of approvals, and a recommendation for further study of domestic partner benefits had survived. I had a sense HR was less than enthusiastic about the idea of offering the benefits. Years later I learned that the discussions at the leadership team level had been contentious, and some were vehemently in opposition to extending domestic partner benefits. If the Shell leadership team were to have voted on whether to offer the benefits, domestic partner benefits would have lost.

It was the CEO who shot down the recommendation for further study of domestic partner benefits. With the facts in hand about corporate trends and the value and costs associated with domestic partner benefits, he made the call. His response—the issue had been studied long enough and the benefits should be implemented. The whole process for getting the domestic partner benefits had taken a little under a year. It would take several more months to incorporate them into the overall compensation and benefits package. People would be eligible to sign up for the domestic partner benefits beginning in January 1998.

I shared with SEA Shell members that the battle had been won and benefits would be offered to both same-sex and unmarried heterosexual couples. Everyone respected a request to keep the news quiet until an official announcement came out. I couldn't believe we'd done it—the efforts of so many people had actually paid off.

Adding to the saga, I was in the middle of breaking up with my boyfriend. You're probably wondering how I had ever found time for a boyfriend. Obviously I hadn't. Let's just say all the stuff going on at the time made for some very long days, and I needed to get away.

I booked a trip to the Netherlands to visit some friends. While there I checked e-mail every couple of days. The morning of Queen's Day I was going through messages and came upon one from Chevron. The Chevron GLBT network leader wanted to share that they had just announced domestic partner benefits. I congratulated him on yet another milestone. I knew Shell was going to offer them, but couldn't share the news at the time.

HR spent another couple months weaving domestic partner health and pension benefits into the new benefits book. SEA Shell had offered to help as a sounding board, but HR chose not to utilize the network as a resource. So when the benefits came out, the SEA Shell benefits sub-committee read through the book, compiled questions about the benefits, and sent them off to HR. HR would respond back and SEA Shell would forward the information to the membership and post it on their internal website. If you can't be a resource to the system, be a resource for your membership.

The *Houston Chronicle* took note of Shell's extending domestic partner benefits by placing a small story on the front page of the business section of the paper. In preparation for any inquiries, I partnered with Media Relations, who were ready and waiting with talking points and statements in hand. They received virtually no negative mail resulting from the story. Media Relations was very proactive and great to work with.

The GLBT weekly paper, the *Houston Voice*, had also done a short story. The response from the community was very receptive. Friends from the GLBT Chamber and other companies sent notes saying they had seen the article and were going to be more selective about where they bought gas.

Around Christmas time, SEA Shell members received an invitation to a weekend gathering at a home in the Rice Village area. Vickie and Clyde, the couple hosting the event, were having a domestic partner benefits affidavit signing party. Those Shell employees and their partners could sign up for the benefits during the party. There were more than just SEA Shell people attending, as more than a hundred people crowded into the house. That day Vickie and Clyde and five other couples signed up for the benefits. I wasn't among them—boyfriends seemed to come and go in my life. My first love has been the intensity of a challenge. That is where I placed most of my time and energy. The intensity of the challenge in finding a boyfriend never seemed to endure with my career challenges. I met some very beautiful men over the years with whom I fell in love, and still love. Yet the intensity was never there.

Prior to the event I found myself dwelling on all the crap we'd gone through to get to that point, and I had to wonder if it was all worth it. Then during the party, when the six couples sat down in the living room to complete their affidavits, I realized it was worth it. Had the effort not been made and the good fight not been fought, there would not have been a party. All the efforts expended over the past eighteen months had culminated in their lives being just a little bit better. They were the first and there would be many more to follow.

There were several points I took away in the pursuit of domestic partnership benefits:

- Relationships are important for building the partnerships necessary to create change in the workplace. I've spent most of my adult life learning and appreciating the value people bring to the table—one of my personal core values.

- One doesn't have to be an extrovert to lead—the challenge for me has always been about overcoming shyness. When opportunities presented themselves, I had to find the self-discipline to say what needed to be said clearly and effectively.

- SEA Shell's greatest strength has always been its members. The ability to engage leaders and effectively influence change and build support from straight allies required the efforts of as many members as possible. Being recognized by the company and supported by the Diversity Center made all the difference in the early days of SEA Shell's development.

- There are going to be those who oppose domestic partner benefits because of their personal beliefs. While I respect their beliefs, I don't want to be governed by them—I have my own values and beliefs, as does everyone. In the workplace I want to be treated with dignity and respect.

Domestic partner benefits extend to same-sex couples some of the same dignities afforded heterosexual couples (e.g. health benefits, caring for an ill partner, funeral leave, etc.).

- Meeting the person vs. the IT president was important to the growth and development of the leader. Leaders need to be on a personal journey if they hope to develop the skills and knowledge necessary to be comfortable with business decisions addressing tough workplace topics like sexual orientation or gender identity.

- A role for a GLBT employee network can be offering opportunities for people to begin coming out at work (e.g. participation in workshops, meetings with leaders, community venues, etc.).

- As in the case with the IT president, ground rules can be an effective method of defining what level of exposure a person may be subject to in a particular venue and allowing the individual the option of choosing his or her level of exposure.

- If you can't be a resource to the system, be a resource to the members of the network. SEA Shell wasn't invited to the table during the final drafting of the new benefits guidebook, but they reviewed the book when it came out, solicited questions from members, and posted the answers on the SEA Shell website.

- Celebrate the successes—sometimes they may feel like they are few and far between. By taking some time to celebrate successes, I began to realize the efforts were making the lives of other people a little easier.

I had the opportunity to check on the number of participants taking advantage of domestic partner benefits a few months after they were implemented and again a couple of years later. Within a few months of offering the benefits, 120 couples had signed up, one-third of which were same-sex couples. By 2000 the number of employees signed up for the benefits had risen to about 180, maintaining the one-third split for same-sex couples. These figures are consistent with other benchmarking data developed by the Human Rights Campaign (HRC) and the Society of Human Resource Managers (SHRM).

An interesting observation from SHRM was a growing number of students asking campus recruiters if their companies offered domestic partner benefits. The question wasn't coming from openly gay students entering the workforce, but from straight students who considered the benefits an indicator of whether a company was progressive.

7 Learning to Walk

There were two key people who joined my life while I was working on the challenges of obtaining domestic partner benefits: a new love, Slava, and Elizabeth Birch, a role model I had long admired. I was also really beginning to understand and appreciate the value of mentors—Judy and Richard continued to be guiding forces molding a young leader.

Vacationing in the Netherlands in the spring of 1997, I met Slava. He was working for a small hotel in Amsterdam. Given the geographic distance, we decided to spend some time getting acquainted before jumping into anything too quickly. So began the long-distance relationship. We both had good jobs, but neither offered the option of living together on the same continent.

As you may have guessed, Slava is not Dutch, but Russian. He moved to the Netherlands, where he had family, in the early '90s shortly after the fall of the Iron Curtain. He was both intrigued and confused by my work on GLBT workplace issues—understandably so for someone living in a country with some very liberal laws. In the Netherlands gay people can serve openly in the military, and it was the first country to recognize same-sex marriage.

We ran up some very hefty phone bills over the first couple of months and decided to get back together for his birthday in early August. I flew over for a week, Slava met me at the airport, and we split our time between his apartment in The Hague and touring Amsterdam. This was the first of many trips that we've taken over the years—back and forth across the ocean, because U.S. law does not recognize our relationship.

For the first year, the travel burden was mine. I didn't mind because I had never taken the time to explore Europe. For our first Valentine's Day, I surprised Slava by going over to see him. He then surprised me by upping the ante—he arranged a few days for us in Paris.

My job was U.S.-centric, offering just three weeks of vacation, which I stretched as much as possible, and I took advantage of a Shell program allowing employees to buy an additional week. I managed several short trips abroad, scheduling well in advance and searching for cheap airfares. This literally became a hobby, as we spent thousands of dollars on phone bills and plane tickets.

The distance made the time we spent separated difficult. Every time I left, a tearful Slava would give me a hug and a kiss at Schipol. It was agonizing to part, leaving him there with tears streaming down his cheeks. After the first few trips I noticed a change in Slava's behavior—the day or two before my departure he would get mad over some of the silliest things. When I asked what was causing the mood swings, he explained they were driven by the reality that I was again getting on a plane and leaving him.

Around the same time I met Slava, I also met Elizabeth Birch, who was the executive director for the Human Rights Campaign (HRC). Under her leadership HRC was quickly becoming the largest GLBT civil rights group in the country. Elizabeth was in town to speak at the Houston HRC Dinner. The Texas Commerce Bank (now JP Morgan Chase) GLBT employee network group had asked her to speak and invited employee network groups from other companies to attend.

Someone needed to pick up Elizabeth at the hotel and shuttle her to and from the speaking engagement at the bank. The materials and tools found on the HRC website had influenced much of my early learning about GLBT workplace issues. Having the chance to spend thirty minutes with Elizabeth before and after the speaking event was a chance I didn't want to miss. So I jumped at the opportunity to play chauffeur and got the job.

During the drive to the meeting we became acquainted. Elizabeth was interested in my background, my life growing up on a dairy in upstate New York, my path to Houston and coming out. We talked about Shell's changing the non-discrimination policy to include sexual orientation, my writing my story for *Out Smart* magazine, and my efforts in building an employee network and working toward domestic partner benefits. Having been with Apple, she could relate to the corporate workplace, and we became engrossed in conversation.

After the presentation I drove Elizabeth back to the hotel. She explored my interest in the HRC, and I confessed that my heart was with workplace issues more than politics, raising money, or black-tie dinners. Elizabeth inquired about the struggle for domestic partner benefits—I was pretty certain we were going to get them, but had no hard data. So I just smiled and promised her a dozen roses when Shell announced the benefits.

In the summer, when the announcement of domestic partner benefits hit the papers, I called the florist and placed an order for a dozen roses. I thought yellow was appropriate given they were coming from Texas. The note said, "*Elizabeth, as promised. Shell announced DP benefits today.*" I received a thank-you call and discovered that yellow roses were her favorite.

Unbeknownst to me at the time, HRC was exploring the creation of a business council comprised of leaders from various business sectors and across the country to be a resource on developing their workplace tools and strategy. The position would require an investment of time and some travel. Participants were not expected to represent their company, just bring their experiences from creating change in the workplace. This was a very exciting proposition.

Because of our conversations in the car a few months earlier, I had attracted Elizabeth's attention. She knew who I was and what I had achieved, and she thought I would make a good candidate for the business council. After a phone call from Elizabeth, I received an invitation to join the business council late in the summer of 1997.

Judy and I discussed the HRC Business Council position at some length. She considered it a very good growth opportunity and suggested exploring whether the Corporate Diversity Center would pick up my expenses. Given the HRC structure, the diversity director thought it prudent to speak with the Government Affairs organization. While they didn't see an issue with my participation, they were noncommittal about whether the Diversity Center should pick up my travel and expenses. Given the response from Government Affairs and assurances from HRC that the Business Council would be domiciled under the Foundation portion of their governance structure, Judy agreed to pick up the costs.

Judy was also concerned about my health and well-being. I had a demanding full-time job, SEA Shell, the Technologies Center Diversity Council, and a boyfriend in Europe. Burnout was a real concern. I assured her I was fine and taking a monastic approach to the workplace, basically giving up personal endeavors to pursue a full plate at Shell. Work was becoming my life—even my friends noticed and shared that it was time for me to find a hobby.

I bounced the business council position off Richard Wiederholt, who told me to take it or he'd kick my butt—strong words for Richard. In his mind, only good things could come out of this opportunity. While I had reservations about being up for the challenge, he had nothing but confidence in my ability to succeed in the position.

With Richard's oversight, I had just pulled together a second article for *Out Smart* magazine documenting how my life had changed since coming out in the workplace almost three years prior. He saw the business council as a huge breakthrough for my growth and development as a community leader, and just another example of how my original story had changed my life.

Slava wasn't completely sure what to make of the invitation to join the Business Council. He really had no context to understand the potential significance. He did offer me what I needed most of all—genuine interest and support. The first Business Council meeting was held in Washington, D.C. just before the first HRC national dinner. I really wanted Slava to meet me there, but he wasn't able to arrange time off from work to fly over, so I went to the event alone.

The HRC Business Council is a book unto itself, and I'm not prepared to be the author. This was a different venue than any I had been exposed to before. I found the people to be extraordinary. As the meeting came to order, we began with self-introductions. I was feeling a little insecure, thinking I had made a big mistake—most had backgrounds as executives, some were pioneers in the GLBT civil rights movement, others were business owners. Across the table from me was the executive VP of diversity for IBM. To my left was the retired vice chairman of Ford Motors. Others brought their workplace knowledge from brand name companies like Bell Atlantic (now Verizon), American Airlines, Wells Fargo, Walgreens, and Bank Boston (now part of Bank of America). I was the only participant from the oil and gas sector.

I began my introduction by speaking about my coming out process, which I had begun three years prior, and the changes in Shell that had followed. As I spoke there were expressions of astonishment and approval from some of my colleagues. It was at that moment I realized why I was there—a company in the conservative oil and gas sector was changing.

A friend in Shell summed it up best when he said, "Very few people have an opportunity to leave their signature on a company, and you've done that through your work on GLBT workplace issues." I was surprised by his words; leaving a signature on a company wasn't what I had set out to do. I just wanted to create a safe, open work environment where people could achieve their potential.

Now I was ready to share my experiences through the HRC Business Council's efforts to leave their signature on corporate America. I had been a member of HRC for years, but had never gained an appreciation for the breadth of their work until joining the Business Council. The Business Council was a potential vehicle to facilitate driving change in corporate America. The initial focus of the Business Council included the following:

- Helping to pass the Employment Nondiscrimination Act (ENDA) by leveraging the skills and competencies of the Business Council members, and increasing the number of companies endorsing the legislation.
- Workplace counseling on GLBT issues, working with employee network groups, business leaders, and others to provide basic guidance.
- Examination of various federal issues that affect GLBT employees in the workplace, like taxation of domestic partner benefits and proxy statements for shareholder resolution.

I've worked on many teams, and none have been as impressive or professional, or possessed such a sense of camaraderie, as the HRC Business Council. Once I got past the titles and positions, the participants were people who were interested in the well-being of others and who wanted to create change in the workplace. This seemed to be the mortar that bonded the group.

Returning from the meeting, I shared with Judy, Richard, Slava and SEA Shell what I had seen and heard. Bill Clinton made history as the first sitting American President to address a GLBT organization by keynoting the HRC National dinner. A couple of thousand people warmly welcomed him to the stage. A number of companies signed on as sponsors of the event. My desire was for Shell to one day be among them. No one in Shell seemed to take issue with my involvement on the Business Council, but it was clear they weren't going to be leading the charge or carrying the banner for creating change. Sexual orientation was still a new topic for many in the business.

Until a strong education program on sexual orientation was in place, it would be difficult for leaders to be comfortable with GLBT workplace issues. Getting the education component to take root was a challenge. For example, a consideration by the president of the Shell IT business when he met with SEA Shell had been setting up an awareness session for the senior leaders of Shell. The topic died on the vine a few months later when the president of the IT business elected to retire.

The Technology Center was well underway with their diversity awareness sessions for all managers, including a module on sexual orientation. The Chemicals business was showing interest in understanding their workforce diversity issues, commissioning a consultant to conduct a series of focus groups. With a little effort I was able to find enough SEA Shell members willing to meet with the consultant at an offsite location and share their perspectives.

What kept sexual orientation off the table as an education topic? The Shell businesses felt they weren't ready to tackle such a difficult subject. More pressing issues pertaining to visible facets of diversity (i.e. race and gender) took precedence. If sexual orientation were going to be a part of the learning curriculum, SEA Shell was going to have to put it there.

SEA Shell was also going through significant changes and showing signs of growing pains. When the network formed, there were a half dozen people meeting offsite in a living room plotting the course. After the diversity director came on board, the meetings were moved into the workplace, typically near the end of the day. SEA Shell had a formal committee structure in place, governance guidelines were created, membership was growing, community outreach interest was growing, and SEA Shell was celebrating the network's first anniversary. Had there not been tangible indicators of change, I think the number of people stepping forward to help build the success of the network would have been much smaller. Having a sense of what others were wrestling with in their decision-making process about coming out, I appreciated and admired their courage.

A number of people staffed various sub-committees. The initial governance model called for a steering team with about 12 or 15 members, which became the real workhorse for the network. The first steering committee really had no elected leaders—my colleague from IT and I were de facto co-chairs.

The group behaved more like a self-governing team, which had its share of benefits and shortcomings. The benefits were a structure promoting consensus building, a shared ownership of the mission and goals, a better distribution of workload, shared responsibility for the reputation and brand of the network, and a shared accountability for successes and failures. The disadvantages included not everyone being well versed in the workings of self-governing teams; at times decision-making was cumbersome, and consensus did not necessarily mean we had a commitment from everyone. Add to all this the desire of the Corporate Diversity Center to have one focal point for the network.

Originally the de facto co-chairs shared the responsibility of being the focal point for the Corporate Diversity Center. Over time, though, my co-chair's assignment changed and he accepted relocation to Brunei, making it impossible to retain his role with SEA Shell. I tried to find a replacement from the steering team to no avail. There were plenty of capable people. The issue was never about finding another person, but rather their ability to meet with the diversity director, whose schedule would shift literally overnight with ever-evolving priorities. As a result, it was difficult for other steering team members to be nimble enough to keep up. At this stage, I made SEA Shell my highest priority at work, becoming the regular point person for the network with the Corporate Diversity Center.

The focus of SEA Shell was profoundly important to me personally, becoming a career priority. Yet at times the pain of being a de facto leader deflected my passion for SEA Shell. I was learning alongside everyone else, and that meant sometimes I got it right and sometimes I fell off the bike.

Others couldn't make the GLBT network a similar priority, and I tried to respect their positions. For most, every moment of time had to be tied to a charge code, and businesses generally didn't have one for employee network time. I had negotiated an arrangement with my management and had performance goals tied to my involvement in diversity and SEA Shell, but other Shell businesses were not as far along in their embracing of diversity.

The position of the Corporate Diversity Center was for the businesses to pick up a portion of the time employees worked on network activities, and the employees would volunteer some of their personal time. Some employee network business (e.g. awareness workshops, contacting nonprofits, meetings with management, participating in company sponsored events, etc.) had to occur during regular business hours. If the business wouldn't pick up the cost, the Corporate Diversity Center would attempt to assist in coming up with an arrangement.

The issue of billable time was not unique to SEA Shell—as other employee networks formed, they too raised the issue. Ultimately the key players in the networks were those most in need of a time sharing agreement, which was a very small portion of the overall employees on the distribution lists.

The Corporate Diversity Center had requested all networks to provide a budget forecast for the coming year, and a list of potential community outreach opportunities. When the steering team met to discuss what SEA Shell should submit for its first budget, there were a number of questions. What was the format? What activities should the network pursue? What should be the focus of community outreach efforts?

Not being given much in the way of structure, my recommendation for the budget format was to tie activities back to the business case. If we wanted to have a chance of securing funding, our efforts had to be of value to the businesses. To this end the format I put forth was comprised of five columns:

- **The work activity** (e.g. creating a website, team building, survey, annual meeting, etc.)
- **Description of activities** (i.e. bullets of what the work actually entails)
- **Benefit to the business**—a short narrative of how the effort supports the diversity goals/ business objectives of Shell
- **The cost** (e.g. materials, fees, travel, registration, labor, etc.)
- **Timing**—when the activities would be achieved.

The outreach portion of the budget posed other challenges. How should we get off on the right foot with the GLBT community? How would we strategically manage the investment, realizing social investment can be more than just philanthropy (e.g. identifying key stakeholders, building relationships, identifying strategic opportunities, positively impacting the economic development of the community, enhancing the company brand and reputation, and establishing appropriate metrics)?

The fact that Shell leadership was not well-versed on the GLBT community was a reasonable starting assumption. Leveraging relationships with leaders, I began exploring acceptable first alternatives for outreach that might also be learning venues. Most seemed interested in low risk entry points to the community that aligned with their business objectives (e.g. attracting and retaining talent, increasing market share, etc.). Once entry points were identified, they would establish a stable foothold for the company to learn and further grow in support of the community.

One way this worked was through involvement with the GLBT Chamber of Commerce. I was aware the Chamber was planning a GLBT business expo, "Empower," for the fall of 1997. The Chamber had aspirations of making Empower an annual event that would profile GLBT-owned and friendly businesses to the community. The business case for Shell participation was easy—opportunity to grow market share. Utilizing the contacts I had made earlier in the year through the awareness workshop with the marketing organization, I sent a letter to the marketing vice president making a case for business sponsorship of the event.

About a week later I received a call from someone in Marketing requesting more details about Empower. After the conversation, Marketing agreed to go with a sponsorship and booth, but they weren't sure how to handle the staffing. I suggested having SEA Shell members in the booth—they knew the community and would be the perfect ambassadors.

The Chamber was very excited about signing on a major oil company as a corporate sponsor. They offered up the best location for the booth, near the entrance of the expo. Everyone entering Empower couldn't miss it. Members of SEA Shell volunteered to be at the booth throughout the exhibition.

During my shift, an older gentleman stopped by the booth. He was a retiree of Shell. Seeing his former employer front and center at Empower was quite a shock. He shared that he'd never thought he'd see the day when Shell would sponsor and visibly participate in a GLBT community event. He was one of many that walked through the expo that day, stopping to voice support. Many said seeing the booth at Empower would be something they'd keep in mind the next time they needed to fill their car.

From 1997 through 2005, Shell remained a sponsor of Empower, and each year they gave out Shell credit card applications.

While I'm not aware of the marketing organization tracking the applications, it would be a good metric for assessing the event's contribution to market share. Another might be assessing the vitality of Shell stations versus competitors in the GLBT areas of the city (i.e. the Montrose and Heights).

Health issues for the GLBT community were another area where support could translate into responsible corporate citizenship and help sustain a vital health services infrastructure for the community. My tendency was to gravitate toward the HIV/AIDS community, overlooking the needs of women and transgender people. Applying a lens of diversity to the GLBT community, a microcosm of society, can create a broader reputation impact for the company. A number of nonprofit GLBT health organizations benefited over the years: AssistHers, AIDS Foundation Houston, The Lesbian Health Initiative, People with AIDS (PWA), and the Miss Camp America Foundation, among others.

I should also clarify that it wasn't up to me as a leader to pick the groups receiving funding. My role was to guide the discussions influencing the creation of a framework for selecting a broad portfolio of charities representing the diversity of the community.

Different venues present different challenges—one example that comes to mind is sponsorship of Miss Camp America. A SEA Shell member had approached me about whether the company would make a contribution to the Miss Camp America Foundation, which raised tens of thousands of dollars annually for various Houston based HIV/AIDS charities. Miss Camp America was an elaborate drag show satiric of the Miss America Beauty pageant and held the same night—the state that won Miss America also won Miss Camp. The event had been entertaining sellout crowds in Houston for over 30 years.

I suggested that the SEA Shell member pull together a briefing package and run it by the Corporate Diversity Center. His package was effective—I heard shortly after our conversation that the Diversity Center was making a $5,000 contribution. Because

Shell was considered a corporate sponsor, the organizers wanted someone to be on stage presenting the check. No one from the Diversity Center or leadership was available, so the duty was delegated to me in my role as de facto leader of SEA Shell. I shared the news with the rest of SEA Shell. The organizers had provided a few VIP passes for SEA Shell steering team members and their partners to attend.

I also told Slava the news. He was in Europe at the time and couldn't come over for the show. It was common during much of our first year together for Slava to be unable to attend special events with me in the States. He was responsible for managing a small hotel in Amsterdam and couldn't just leave when an event came up for me in the U.S. All I could do was tell him about it over the phone and send him a copy of the video they had given me.

The night of the show, I donned a suit and placed a picture of Slava in the jacket pocket near my heart for luck. That year the show was titled "Under the Big Top," playing on a circus theme. After the introductory overtures, the ringmaster announced the Shell sponsorship and introduced me to present the check. I did have a few prepared remarks, which I had memorized, and I had hard copy in my pocket next to the picture of Slava just in case I fumbled. I'd never been on stage before in front of 1,500 people. Just three minutes on stage, three rounds of applause and a standing ovation—not bad. My remarks were short:

> One of Shell's core values is belief in people, but can people really make a difference? In a little over a year I've seen Shell add sexual orientation to its nondiscrimination policy; employee groups have been forming, one of which is SEA Shell, Shell's gay and lesbian group; and just recently an announcement was made that effective January of 1998 Shell will be extending domestic partner benefits to eligible employees.

> These are many changes over a very short period of time. They didn't occur because of a corporate whim, but because of people and their ability to make a difference. This trend continues here tonight with Shell's sponsorship of a very worthwhile event, the Miss Camp America pageant.
>
> Because we are a Texas oil company and everything in Texas is big, it's my honor and privilege to present you with this check on behalf of Shell's gay and lesbian community. It's a check from Shell Oil Company to the Miss Camp America Foundation for $5,000.

This marked the first time Shell Oil Company had publicly made a donation to a gay organization. For months afterward people would stop by my table in restaurants or on the street to say thanks for the check from Shell and their gay and lesbian employees. Several employees in the audience that night sent complimentary notes to the CEO, sharing the experience through their eyes. The one-night event raised over $80,000 for various HIV/AIDS charities.

A few days after the event, however, the climate started to change, like a storm front moving in off the Gulf. As the story was relayed to me, a freelance reporter for a small publication in the oil and gas industry had written a story supporting Shell's contribution to the event. However, when the story came out it did more to sensationalize the event and was considered unflattering by some company leaders. Suddenly the Diversity Center found itself in the midst of managing the story, the concern being what competitors might think on reading the article.

While the magazine was not viewed as a major source of news in the oil and gas community, the effect of the story internally was very much the "mouse that roared." The upstream part of the oil and gas industry has long been viewed as a bastion of conservatism. A great deal of time and energy was invested in briefing the leaders and preparing media responses. As I thought a leader should, I accepted full responsibility for the event and a willingness to do whatever necessary to help work through the issues.

The lesson for me? This was too big of an outreach step given where Shell was in their understanding of the community at the time. Being successful in establishing a meaningful relationship between Shell and the community would mean having to find more moderate venues, at least for the time being. As leaders became more comfortable with the community and its activities, other vehicles could be explored.

An unanticipated feature of the Miss Camp America event was strengthening the communication links between SEA Shell and the company. Media Relations and I formulated responses to possible inquiries about sponsorship of the event, which provided elements of how a communication strategy for the network could unfold.

Occasionally calls would come in from external media sources about various aspects of Shell's effort in the GLBT community. When the calls came in they were directed first to Media Relations to have the inquiry logged in. Media Relations would then help facilitate the interview process, assuring that knowledgeable people on the topic addressed the request. For example, the call might come back to SEA Shell or possibly be redirected to Corporate Affairs, Human Resources or the Corporate Diversity Center.

Interactions with the diversity director were building my aptitude and experience working with the executive level of a company. This was a different experience than the training I had been doing in the past with other executives. In this situation I was being tested on my organizational skills, ability to present points concisely and objectively, and offer recommendations that were balanced and sound.

An example of a development opportunity occurred when employee network leaders were summoned to a meeting hosted by the Corporate Diversity Center to participate on a sounding board for business leaders addressing a workplace issue. The infraction involved employees from two of the businesses. The two businesses summarized what had occurred and offered recommendations. The network leaders and others in the room were then asked to formulate a consensus on how the issues should be resolved. This was a revolutionary concept—senior leaders utilizing grassroots leaders in the company to partner in reasoning through an issue and formulating a response.

This was one of my earliest experiences in observing how trust between business leaders and employee networks could cultivate a strong foundation for the betterment of the company. It was also an example of the power of networks and how they could be leveraged to partner with and support the businesses. The result was a well-thought-out course of action calling for appropriate discipline.

Through various internal media channels, the reputation of SEA Shell eventually spanned the Atlantic to the UK, where a gay employee sent a white paper to the business leaders just prior to his retirement from the company. I gave him a call and discovered a loose-knit group of GLBT employees existed in Shell UK. Our conversation led to others, and before long I had discovered another group of GLBT employees in Shell Netherlands.

My first reaction was to bring them into SEA Shell and expand our sphere of influence across the "pond." That didn't sit well with the Corporate Diversity Center. In 1997 Shell Oil Company still behaved as a U.S. subsidiary of the parent, Royal Dutch/ Shell Group (the Group). A three-person team was addressing diversity at the group level. While employee networks were being embraced in the U.S., they were not a part of the strategy on the other side of the pond.

That didn't mean I couldn't stay in touch with the people in London and The Hague. Although they were not formally part of SEA Shell, we did include them on our distribution list, keeping them apprised of our efforts in the U.S. Whenever I had a business opportunity that took me to the Netherlands, I made a point of trying to get together with some of my GLBT colleagues there.

Riding my learning curve, I often pondered where best to focus energy to expand my knowledge of community and issues. There was help—Richard had no shortage of ideas for my development. One day he called and asked for my biography. When I inquired as to the urgency he replied, "You're running for the board of the Greater Houston GLBT Chamber of Commerce." To which I replied, "I am?" Suddenly, I was campaigning to GLBT Chamber members to become part of the board. In November the results were tallied, and I was on the board.

The goals I had established for my campaign would be the focus of my two-year assignment:

- Pursue opportunities for promoting community partnering between Houston's corporations and the GLBT community.

- Explore and develop opportunities to leverage the broad diversity of the GLBT community to enhance their economic growth and vitality.

The first goal really targeted networking the various corporate GLBT employee groups existing in Houston. There weren't many in 1997: Southwestern Bell, Texas Commerce Bank (now JP Morgan Chase), Exxon (now ExxonMobil), Shell, and Amoco (now BP). Another facet was influencing Shell to join the Chamber. After all, they were members of other chambers in the city, so why not this one?

The second goal proved to be more daunting. While community events and planning meetings are open to all, representation from various minority groups can be lacking among the rank and file of those attending. When possible, I encouraged outreach by the Chamber to include minorities. To their credit, they've steadily made progress in this area over the years.

The board position opened my eyes to what chambers do for business and community. As I developed a better sense of the

GLBT community, Chamber members obtained a better appreciation of Shell. For all practical purposes I was an ambassador to the community. Eventually, through the relationship I nurtured, Shell Chemical joined the fold of GLBT Chamber sponsors. They supported the underwriting of the Chamber's newsletter during the early development years of the organization.

As the journey continued, so did my growth and development, both personally and professionally:

- Slava was different from anyone else I had dated. As our relationship evolved, we became very adept at maximizing time together. We thought it prudent to become more acquainted before tackling the hurdles posed by U.S. laws and institutions that kept us physically apart. Living on separate continents takes a toll on any relationship.

- Sometimes the most menial tasks can lead to great opportunities. Had I not taken the time to drive Elizabeth Birch to the meeting hosted by Texas Commerce (Chase) Bank, we might not have had the opportunity to talk about the changes occurring in the workplace at Shell, a conversation that led to my appointment to the HRC Business Council.

- The HRC Business Council was an opportunity to meet and learn from executives who were gay, lesbian or supportive of the GLBT cause. Meeting them in the context of the HRC Business Council helped me shed the stigma that titles create in the workplace. The experience also showed I could play on a national level when it came to GLBT workplace issues.

- Judy and Richard provided valuable insights and perspectives for my growth and development. Both stepped in where they felt a need to facilitate the furthering of my learning process. Judy supported my involvement on the

HRC Business Council, and Richard motivated my rise to the board of the Greater Houston GLBT Chamber of Commerce.

- Leaving a signature on Shell was never a motive for the work I pursued on my journey of being out in the workplace. I just wanted to create a safe, open work environment where people could achieve their potential.
- Having a charter and structure for the employee network group was important to the success of SEA Shell. Clearly articulating a mission and goals and identifying subcommittees empowered members to influence change.
- Defining a budget and outreach strategy proved critical to helping the company understand the business value of an employee network. My role was to facilitate others to derive the possibilities supporting the mission and goals of SEA Shell and how they aligned with the objectives of the businesses.
- Having a good working relationship and credibility with Media Relations and other key internal organizations proved invaluable when developing responses to internal/external reactions to outreach efforts.
- When the going got tough, I was willing to accept responsibility. It's easy for people to criticize actions or shift blame, but this posture doesn't move anyone toward a solution or support a constructive learning environment.
- The institutions may inhibit the expansion and creation of a global employee network, but they probably don't prevent the building of meaningful relationships or the ability to learn from and support each other.
- By building credibility, grassroots leaders could effectively partner with senior business leaders in building consensus

on resolving some tough workplace situations, such as crafting appropriate interventions addressing behaviors based on difference.

8 Adapting to Change

Everything up to this point in my life was the "foundation" years. The board positions expanded my network of connections in the community, along with my knowledge and understanding of the evolution of the community and its desires. The HRC Business Council was honing my leadership skills and competencies—challenging my thinking and mental models of how I viewed executives. A question for me shifted from how to get leaders to work sexual orientation into their learning portfolio, to how to help them learn about workplace issues given all the other demands made upon their time by the business.

A shift also occurred in my life—I was being recognized for my contributions as a change agent. The company was beginning to garner recognition for their efforts to create a more equitable work environment. These were the "recognition" years—as my network of people grew, so did my notoriety. This was something I hadn't really anticipated—my intention was not to become the "poster boy" for SEA Shell or GLBT workplace issues. I think my friends and colleagues would describe me as most comfortable behind the scenes, influencing strategy and direction. But creating meaningful change was causing me to stand out whether I liked it or not.

Recognition for Shell began when a member of the Houston HRC Steering Committee relayed that Shell had been selected to receive the HRC Corporate Equality Award. I passed the information along to the Corporate Diversity Center. They were happy to have me accept the award on behalf of Shell, but my day job had me other places. I couldn't rearrange my schedule for the award, and no one else from the SEA Shell steering team was available. So a member of the Corporate Diversity Center accepted on behalf of Shell.

In early 1998 Shell issued their first Diversity Progress Report. The issue featured an article summarizing the efforts of the employee networks and how they fit into the overall strategy for diversity. With the article was a picture of me and other network leaders. The report was the first company-wide communication associating me with the GLBT employee network—if I wasn't out before, I was now.

My first reaction to seeing the document was to brace for a backlash and hate mail—to my astonishment, it never came. Colleagues at Westhollow who saw the article were very supportive and complimentary. If anyone took issue with Shell's embracing sexual orientation under the umbrella of diversity and inclusion, they weren't directing the criticism in my direction. I think this was attributed to the strong position Judy and her management team had taken on wanting a respectful and inclusive work environment.

The publicity created by the story had other positive consequences—SEA Shell was receiving more inquiries from prospective members. Among employees wanting to join SEA Shell were a number of straight allies. The addition of straight allies to the mix made it easier for GLBT members to be visible at SEA Shell events—no one could assume that all members of SEA Shell were GLBT.

I was receiving more inquiries to be a resource to managers and others in various parts of the company. For instance, a few weeks after the Diversity Progress Report, I received a call from someone in the Corporate Diversity Center wanting to explore my thoughts on the creation of a religious employee network. My initial reaction was suspicion and alarm—one could not be discriminated against because of religion under federal law, and Christianity is the dominant religious group in the U.S. Why would an "advantaged" group need an employee network?

As I thought about it, I realized that Christians were not exactly a repressed group in the U.S., but other religious groups were (e.g. Muslims, Hindus, Jews, etc.). If a network were formed under the premise of raising awareness of workplace issues for various religious groups, there might be a case for action.

As the viability of a religious network was examined further, the interested parties seemed to prefer a Christian network to one for all religious groups. Given that the Christian population of the company already had an extensive network of Bible study groups and they were not a historically repressed group, the formalization of a Christian network seemed unnecessary.

This is a topic a number of companies have wrestled with over the years, with some actually recognizing the creation of religious networks. My opinion on the subject was that I thought a group could be viable if it were inclusive of all religions and, like other networks, was open to anyone. Eventually the interest in the religious network waned. Months later the company cemented a position of not recognizing employee networks formed around religious, social, or political venues.

Among those seeking out SEA Shell was an unusual individual with whom I have struck a long and enjoyable friendship—Ronnie. Ronnie had seen the Diversity Progress Report and sent me an e-mail asking if we could get together. Keeping with my desire to meet everyone in SEA Shell, I agreed and we met for lunch.

Ronnie was an operator in one of the units of the Deer Park chemical plant. His life had become complicated a few years prior when co-workers discovered that he cross-dressed as a woman outside of work. Ronnie was "gender dysphoric" (i.e. not happy with the gender assigned at birth). As he relayed his story and situation in the workplace, I could sense how deeply upset he was. He saw SEA Shell as a possible haven within which to find support and make friends.

The transgender community was a whole new frontier in my learning. Prior to Ronnie, I had met one transgender person who had transitioned from male to female at Amoco (now BP). Friends on the HRC Business Council with American Airlines had talked of people transitioning in their workplace. But I had not personally known someone who was transgender and wanting to transition.

I felt very uncomfortable with Ronnie. He was someone I really didn't know, going through a very personal and profound change in his life. I wasn't in a position to understand, and certainly couldn't relate to or know how he felt. I found out through other conversations with friends that I wasn't alone—others among my gay and lesbian friends and colleagues also struggled with the transgender element of our community.

This is but a brief explanation of the terms used and by no means an exhaustive review. There are many resources available on the web that cover the topics of gender identity/expression and transgender people in much more detail.

Gender identity is a psychological sense of how we see ourselves (i.e. man or woman). As is true with most things in nature, gender identity is not just black or white, nor is everyone born just male or female—some children at birth may be inter-sex (having some of the genitalia for both male and female). Gender expression is a series of socially constructed norms dictating how gender is displayed by our physical appearance (e.g. men wear pants and women wear dresses). Those with gender identities and gender expressions varying from socially constructed norms are considered "transgender".

Ronnie was transgender—a broad term used to include cross-dressers, inter-sexed people, transsexuals, and people living much of their lives as other than their birth gender. Ronnie was transsexual—a transitioning transgender person who modifies his or her physical characteristics and manner of expression to satisfy standards of membership in another gender. For Ronnie the transition was from male to female.

After some reflection I realized that the way I felt after my initial conversation with Ronnie was probably the way most straight people felt after their initial conversations with me. Ronnie's first gift to me was this self-realization, because it affected how I approached others with my work regarding sexual orientation. Straight people were probably experiencing a similar level of discomfort with me when approached for the first time about gay and lesbian issues.

I tend to be uncomfortable with those things I least understand, but with some self-education and awareness those topics are often not be so scary after all. I decided Ronnie had a few things to teach me. I started by having some conversations with his therapist, who explained where people like Ronnie were in their transition and where they were headed. At some point they begin hormone treatments and dress as a woman full time for at least a year before progressing with the surgical reassignment of their gender. The therapist shared insights about transition plans for transsexuals—basically a document outlining next steps and a time line, as well as offering guidance to employers.

This was also a new frontier for the Corporate Diversity Center—while they had reservations about working the transgender issue, the Diversity Center focal point for the networks was open to learning. Ronnie explored with me the possibility of being on the SEA Shell Steering Committee, which I thought was a good idea. Being on the steering committee provided a firsthand learning opportunity for other team members and the network focal point in the Diversity Center.

There were some bumps along the road—SEA Shell had been chartered as a gay and lesbian employee network group open to anyone. During some of the early discussions about naming the network, we had shied away from using the acronym "GLBT."

The original members were gay or lesbian, and if bisexual or transgender employees decided to join, we'd revisit the charter down the road.

Ronnie became the first openly transgender member of SEA Shell, at times dressing as "Sara" for some of the steering team meetings. While some were open to learning, others felt working transgender issues might erode the effectiveness of the network to obtain support from straight allies and make inroads with leaders.

My first sense of how tough the "row would be to hoe" on gender identity came shortly after Ronnie joined the SEA Shell steering team. The Corporate Diversity Center was doing a story on the employee networks for the *Shell News*, a quarterly magazine that was distributed to all employees and retirees of the company. I was interviewed for the story, and a photographer was to drop in on the next steering committee meeting to take a group photo.

The day of the photo shoot, Sara, not Ronnie, attended the meeting. Some people had elected not to be in the photo because they weren't out at work. I had no idea whether Sara would want to be in the picture until the photographer positioned us for the shoot. She was well dressed in professional women's attire. Her hair was brushed and makeup neatly done. She also seemed nervous, not about the photo, but about her debut. This was the first time we had met Sara.

I was sure the Corporate Diversity Center would freak when they saw the photo, and to my surprise that didn't happen. I started to think maybe they were more progressive than I had originally thought. The photo and the article cleared all the reviews. The network liaison from the Corporate Diversity Center and I discussed Sara's being in the photo, and he told me there were no objections in the review process.

When the magazine came out, some of that changed. People at the chemical plant where Sara worked saw the article, recognizing Sara as their co-worker, Ronnie. They generated significant criticism, some of which was relayed to me by colleagues at the

Westhollow Technologies Center. It was as if some people took great delight in making Ronnie's life agony. Suddenly I was thrust into the middle of developing an intervention for the chemical plant in partnership with the Corporate Diversity Center. The event eventually simmered, but it was a keen lesson about how much work there was to do on gender identity in the workplace.

Ronnie was a living, breathing person made of the same flesh and bone as everyone else. He was also a part of the GLBT equation. Like everyone else, all he really wanted was to be treated with dignity and respect, and to feel like he was part of something special. To understand Ronnie, I also had to know "Sara." If I was going to be true to my principles and values, then Sara should have a place at the table along with everyone else. This was going to be a long, uphill learning struggle for the businesses and SEA Shell.

There were other changes on the horizon for SEA Shell. Shell entered into a venture with Texaco, not exactly a leader in diversity at the time. The Shell U.S. CEO announced his retirement plans, and Royal Dutch/Shell had begun the integration of some of the U.S. assets into existing global businesses.

These changes brought challenges for the employee networks. It wasn't clear what impact the restructuring would have on Shell's employee networks—Texaco didn't have them. I was part of the business being amalgamated into the Shell/Texaco venture referred to as the "Alliance" companies. Whether I'd still be able to participate in SEA Shell activities after the Alliance companies formed was up in the air. The Alliance companies would have their own overhead functions, including a Diversity Center.

I heard through my connections that the Alliance companies were going outside to find a diversity director. While attending the Out & Equal Workplace Conference (a conference focusing specifically on GLBT workplace issues) in Rochester, I met a couple of guys from Sears who, upon learning I was from Shell, shared their disappointment over losing their diversity director, Redia.

She had been hired as the Alliance companies' diversity director. The guys attributed their GLBT network's success to Redia's enduring support—with a reference like that, I had to meet her.

After returning to the office, every Monday I'd check the e-mail directory to see if Redia's address had been posted. After a couple of weeks it finally popped up, so I shot off a quick e-mail welcoming her to the company and introducing myself. She replied, suggesting we get together and chat. From there we began building our working relationship—there was no shortage of topics to discuss. We talked about our backgrounds, her work at Sears, my work with SEA Shell and workplace issues, how she saw diversity being positioned in the Alliance companies, and the role of employee networks.

Redia was very supportive of networks and shared how they could be an effective resource for the education of leadership and the businesses. She was just starting to get her arms around the Alliance companies at the time of our first meeting. We agreed to continue periodically getting together to learn from each other. By the end of each session I would have a couple of action items to get back with her on, and she would do the same for me. The action items often focused on continued learning, community contacts, or outreach opportunities.

With an ever-expanding network of contacts to maintain along with other responsibilities, I was becoming drained. Judy's concern that I might reach a burnout point if I didn't do something to distribute the load was becoming a reality. The community board positions, my place on the Technology Center Diversity Council, the HRC Business Council, SEA Shell, Slava and my full-time job were all making demands on my time. Judy was right—things were already slipping through the cracks, I was struggling to concentrate in meetings, and I spent much of my weekends working.

In response to these pressures, I began thinking about my future. I saw a potential opportunity to shift my career a bit and move into a diversity role, where I seemed to excel and found rewarding work. The Westhollow Technology Center Diversity Council had made a recommendation to leadership that a full time diversity manager be hired for the location. I decided to set my sights on pursuing the opportunity.

I was also ready to move out of my role as a leader for SEA Shell, deciding that by the end of 1998 I would no longer be a member of the steering committee. There was enough structure in place for the employee network to elect another leader.

The one piece of the employee network governance model not yet in place was an Executive Advisory Board (EAB). The board was to be comprised of about six to eight senior leaders from across the business—one being a member of the CEO's leadership team. The EAB would function in a review capacity for the network's plans and budget, and help identify and eliminate obstacles to achieving progress in the workplace. The EAB was also a learning opportunity for senior leaders. The members of the EAB for SEA Shell didn't have to be gay or even supportive—just willing to learn.

The Shell diversity director met with the CEO's leadership team to discuss their role in participating on the Executive Advisory Boards. All members of the leadership team could participate on an EAB, with the exception of the CEO. After the CEO's leadership team meeting, I was briefed on the outcome. After discussing the roles of the EAB's, members of the CEO's leadership team were given the opportunity to volunteer for the EAB of their choice. When the dust settled, all of the employee networks had at least one member of the CEO's leadership team, with the exception of SEA Shell.

My heart sank as the story continued: the diversity director had challenged the leaders to consider what made it easier for them to select other networks, but not SEA Shell. For most it was their level of discomfort with GLBT workplace issues. Finally, the new leader for the IT business agreed to be on the EAB for SEA

Shell if someone else would join him—the head of the Shell tax firm then also stepped forward.

My reaction to the whole story was one of disappointment and anger. No one on the CEO's leadership team really seemed to care one way or another about what happened to the GLBT employees in the company. They would probably all be much happier if we just went away. I really wanted to show them up, let them know what it felt like to be treated like a pile of garbage. The message for me from the story was one of rejection—maybe I should just quit and let them have their pathetic company.

Usually when I get angry, my natural response is not to share what I think until I've slept on it. Over the course of the day the pain and anger slowly subsided. I started thinking about what I was going to tell the rest of the SEA Shell steering committee. For better or worse, I was still a part of this "pathetic company." I don't know what made me think the leaders at the top of the organization were going to be any more receptive than anyone else. They were resistant on domestic partner benefits and hadn't demonstrated any interest in learning about GLBT workplace issues. Still, there had to be an opportunity here somewhere.

The silver lining was that two senior leaders had reluctantly stepped forward, expressing a willingness to learn, and I felt they deserved a fair chance. Relaying the story of how they had become SEA Shell's EAB members seemed counterproductive. So rather than sharing the story with the steering committee, I told them only that we had had two senior leaders step forward. At the time SEA Shell was the only network with that level of senior leadership representation. The other steering committee members were very excited, and the news was a real boost for morale.

I did the personal briefing for the two executives, providing them with background information, including SEA Shell's mission, goals, business case, surveys, a summary of current network activities, issues, and accomplishments, and names of other potential EAB members. I didn't share with them my knowledge of how they had arrived on the EAB. Before going into the meeting, I buried the "baggage" of how they were identified for SEA Shell in the back of my mind.

They were very inquisitive, making some recommendations regarding other EAB members on our list. The leader for the IT business shared that he had some "baggage" of his own, but was ready to work with SEA Shell. His inquiries certainly supported his remarks. He asked about the sensitivity of the "coming out" process, the issues faced by employees in the workplace, and the demographics of SEA Shell (i.e. were there any people of color and women?). This demonstrated to me a sincere interest on his part to want to understand how he could help.

The head of the tax firm made me think through the need for his involvement on the EAB. He rationalized that so few of the members of the network were from the firms that it seemed unwarranted. I countered that underrepresentation from the firms was probably a symptom of the workplace climate, a strong justification for his involvement and visibility on the SEA Shell EAB.

I think the decision not to share the narrative of how the leaders had made it onto the EAB was a good choice. I was the only one carrying the "baggage" and would soon be off the SEA Shell steering team. SEA Shell and their EAB became close working partners. I watched the growth and development of the two executives over the years and came to respect and admire their willingness to keep open minds. In time they grew into supporters of GLBT workplace issues, displaying their support in a tangible manner. I was very proud of them and realized why they were leaders.

The scariest part of my transition to a diversity role would be walking away from the career path I had been following for the past thirteen years and going down a completely different road. I had no idea where a new path might take me, but I slowly became comfortable with the notion the change was good. I had to ask myself a question: "Can I become comfortable with the uncertainty a career path change would bring, not knowing where it will take me professionally?"

Richard and I talked extensively about what I was wrestling with, and as always, he had an answer—he reminded me of a book I might want to read again: *Oh, The Places You'll Go!* by Dr. Seuss. Once again I read the book and realized that being afraid of uncertainty was okay, and I had to find the courage to face up to that fear and move on.

There were consequences associated with being an openly gay leader. I was struggling to find my own identity in a straight workplace. Shell was very effective at grooming managers, but not so when it came to leaders, especially if they didn't fit the traditional "mold." To the extent possible, Richard and Judy were helping me discover myself, but there were limitations to what even they could do about my internalized homophobia—the fear of being myself.

I really struggled with the prospect of moving away from a supportive work environment where I was established and comfortable with my identity. My relationship with Slava was progressing, and I wasn't sure a new position would afford being able to find time for each other given the geographic barriers. Another issue was the retirement of our CEO, who had been a champion of diversity—had he not been there, I'm not sure SEA Shell would have made so much progress. More troublesome was whether his successor would be as supportive of diversity. I had no idea whether a new position would continue to allow my participation on the HRC Business Council.

While pondering the future and limiting my universe to the Westhollow Technology Center, something very unexpected happened—the Shell Corporate Diversity Center posted two new positions. I had applied for similar jobs a year prior, but didn't make it past the second round of screening. What made these postings different were calls from people in the Corporate Diversity Center informing me of the job postings in the event I might consider applying. Figuring what the heck, I applied and began moving through the first round of screening. I told Judy and Richard the day I applied and kept them current on each phase of the selection process. I was pretty sure I'd again be knocked out in the second round. To my surprise I was short listed for the third round, and then the fourth.

The final phase was an interview with the corporate diversity director. She asked about my role with SEA Shell and whether I would be willing to step down as their leader. As a diversity consultant I would not be able to retain a leadership role in a network; none of the diversity consultants could because of a possible perception of bias—our role was to be objective. She assured me that the new CEO was very supportive of diversity and saw no reason why I shouldn't continue my involvement with the HRC Business Council.

One final question I recalled from the meeting was about my motivation, and from where did I draw my strength? That was easy—Slava. He was becoming an integral part of my life, and I expressed interest in any opportunities to work on projects in Europe.

Within a couple of weeks the corporate diversity director called and extended an offer. The new assignment began in November, giving me a couple weeks to transition workload at Westhollow. The move also meant a promotion and relocating into the Shell corporate offices downtown—my first assignment in corporate.

Slava had gone back to the Netherlands after spending most of August and September with me in Houston. Arriving home, I gave him a call to break the news. I told him, "You're the second to know." To which he replied, "Second? Who was the first?" When I laughed and said I was the first, he had to laugh as well. He was very excited. We had plans to get together next in a couple of months for the Christmas holiday and would celebrate then.

Slava's trip over was his first time visiting me in Houston. To the extent possible I had carved out time while he was here to meet key people in my life and visit places I enjoyed. Slava had the opportunity to meet Judy and Richard, both of whom were very impressed. As part of the itinerary he attended the second HRC National dinner with me in Washington, D.C. It was nice having him there. When I wasn't in meetings we'd take a stroll around the neighborhoods of Dupont Circle or grab a bite at a quiet cafe.

Transitioning out of the SEA Shell leadership was timely. I was finding myself regularly at odds with others on the steering committee. The steering committee functioned well when it came to managing SEA Shell. Where it seemed to struggle was in the leadership of SEA Shell. A story that bears this point involves the second SEA Shell survey completed in early 1998.

A chronic criticism of the first GLBT workplace survey by managers was that it was open ended in the comments section and not an accurate picture of current reality in the workplace. People were sharing experiences of what had happened to them during their career, some of which were several years old or more. The point to counter this was acknowledging that some of the stories may have been old, but the fact they were sticking in the individual's mind gave testament to the emotional impact created.

Given that the first survey had been done a couple of years prior, the SEA Shell steering committee agreed to pursue another. I had met someone in HR who had expertise in the area of surveys and expressed interest in helping. He provided a cost estimate for the work, which the steering team approved, and I agreed to supervise the work. He started by tightening up the survey questions and solicited the help of a student at the University of Houston to do the actual compilation of the data and comments.

When the surveys came in, I sent them off to the student. I had forgotten that one of the steering team members had begun setting up a format for the survey results to do the data analysis. It had completely slipped my mind until it came up during a project review by the SEA Shell steering team. I apologized for the slip, recommending to the steering team that the student continue the work because of his qualifications. After all, he was under the direction of the person in HR who was experienced in the art of surveys, the costs were part of the budget, and it removed the burden of compiling the data from an already busy steering team.

In response I was pummeled with accusations of mismanaging the survey budget and needing more supervision from my peers. One person even went so far as to say, "How do we know this student is even working on the survey results and not off taking a cruise with our money?" What I couldn't understand was why they were troubled by a qualified professional supervising a student to do the work for a set cost we had all agreed to.

The reason appeared to be a lack of trust. Many on the steering team were from the IT business. They knew each other, interacted on a regular basis, and had built an effective working relationship among themselves. The rest of us were from other businesses and our interactions were limited to steering team and subcommittee interactions.

Another lesson for me was the importance of keeping accurate records of the key decisions being made by the committee. While meeting minutes were available, they often didn't capture the details of key actions. As a result, questions would come up and actions would be revisited on a regular basis. Having grown up on a dairy farm, I refer to this practice as "cud-chewing."

When faced with struggles or frustration, I find myself dwelling on what I've learned from various engagements over the years. Several points have become embedded in my mind over time:

- Sometimes the right answer isn't always the easy answer and may not even be to your personal benefit, but it is still the right answer.
- A person cannot lead meaningful change in an organization from the closet.

- No matter how negative or hostile a situation may seem, look for a positive attribute.
- Never criticize another until you've walked in his or her shoes.
- A true leader shares the credit for a job well done and accepts the responsibility when things go wrong.
- Rather than making demands of leadership on an issue, consider offering suggestions and your services to help find a meaningful resolution.
- When you make a decision, think about what's the best course of action for the whole, not what's best for you personally.
- Life is a journey in learning—keeping learning.

To their credit, the steering team was a viable vehicle for managing the work activities of SEA Shell. Allowing others to take responsibility for a project and run with it was still a stretch. Much of the focus was on administering the structure and systems for getting the work done. They relied on controls, doing things right and managing within the bottom line—all the traits one would want in good managers.

As a team I saw two areas of strength—generating creative ideas and analysis and assessment. If structured properly, a team with these attributes could be very effective. If not structured properly, it could fall into a cycle of idea generation—analysis/ assessment—more idea generation. The outcome of the latter was a team which has trouble focusing on goals and achieving meaningful progress.

In the example of the SEA Shell survey, we came to consensus as a team on the work, but frequently revisited why it was being done and why we were spending the money. The survey was ultimately completed, and the data put to good use.

I cannot stress enough the importance of understanding the dynamics of the team and the different work styles of individual members. With the help of an organizational development consultant, the SEA Shell steering committee participated in a one-day offsite meeting to work through various topics. Knowing the direction my career was about to take, I wove in a piece to address a successor. By the end of the meeting SEA Shell would have officers. The SEA Shell meeting was scheduled for a couple of days after the announcement of my new job assignment and promotion. Everyone in the meeting would know that I was moving into a new role.

Richard and I had dinner the night the announcement came out about my promotion and transfer to the Corporate Diversity Center. Over dinner he gave me a card, asking that I open it later. He thought my career change was a good move and expressed interest about how I was feeling. Pretty nervous, actually. I had no idea where the job might take me in the future. Having been a university professor and shedding that career to become a small business owner, Richard was very familiar with what I was going through. His personal philosophy on life was built on having confidence in yourself and pursuing your hopes and dreams.

I opened the card when I got home. Inside he had written:

> I am really proud of you. You have shown a lot of courage during the last couple of years—and now it's paying off for you. Keep believing in yourself and keep doing "the right thing." You won't regret it. For so many years I have made decisions from my heart and gut instead of my intellect. I have never regretted those decisions. Sometimes we think too much, we analyze too much, and we don't listen to our hearts. I want to live long enough to see what an impact you will have on making this a better world to live in. Maybe it's time for you to re-read your Dr. Seuss book.

Lots of words of wisdom in there. Congratulations! I love you very much—Richard

I never forgot his words, and to this day I still have the card —inserted between the pages of my Dr. Seuss book. When I feel a sense of disorientation in life, I open the book, read the story, and close with reading Richard's card.

A couple of days later I found myself in a room with the rest of the SEA Shell Steering Committee for one last meeting. The facilitator worked through the arduous daylong agenda. After clarification on roles and responsibilities, members of the steering team nominated fellow committee members to various leadership slots. Sara had nominated me for a co-chair position, but I respectfully declined. By the end of the day, SEA Shell and I were free. The network would have to stand on its own, going forward just as I'd have to do with my career. I was very proud of the accomplishments SEA Shell had made and confident the new leadership would continue to do some really great things.

There was an internal peace in letting go—knowing the network would thrive. There was also a void of uncertainty about what role, if any, I would play in the future on GLBT workplace issues. My hope was that my new position in the Corporate Diversity Center would provide some opportunities to grow in this facet of workplace inclusion. I worried about Ronnie, on his own learning journey to become Sara.

Just a little over four years had passed since my coming out at work, and I was still learning things—about others and about myself:

- Although I'm an introvert, I had to learn to be comfortable as an extrovert. I'm most comfortable behind the scenes, influencing strategy and direction. Creating meaningful change was causing me to stand out whether I liked it or not.

- I have a tendency to brace for the worst and hope for the best. My initial response after the publication of the first Shell Diversity report was to brace for an anti-gay backlash—it never came. Instead the report served as a company-wide communication that brought a boost to SEA Shell's membership.
- The topic of a Christian employee network demonstrated my ability to reason through tough issues before rendering an opinion. Not that long ago I might have responded to the same challenge with a quick and decisive opposition.
- The discomfort I was feeling with transgender issues was probably very similar to what straight people felt when I approached them about gay and lesbian issues. If I was going to be comfortable with transgender issues and supportive of Ronnie's transition, I had much to learn.
- The only one who had to be convinced that I was suffering from burnout was myself—it was personally difficult to see the strain of my obligations until things began slipping through the cracks.
- Transitioning SEA Shell would require more than a quick handoff of responsibilities—I felt an obligation to complete unfinished business and structure the handoff with the desire for SEA Shell to be sustainable and thrive.
- Choosing not to share the story of how SEA Shell obtained its first EAB members gave the executives and the steering team the opportunity to enter the room with a clean slate. I would be the only one carrying the baggage.
- At times I felt empowered to do things, but found myself often revisiting agreements and decisions with the steering team. Keeping accurate records of the key decisions being

made by the steering committee was one way of avoiding the "cud-chewing."

- Changing careers was a scary proposition—I found myself pondering the changes and what they might mean. I had to face my fears and concerns and move through them in order to be successful.

That night after the SEA Shell workshop, I lay in bed looking at the ceiling, playing back the day in my mind and reflecting on the past couple of years. With all the preparations for the meeting and the transitioning into the new job, I had completely forgotten what day it was—the four-year anniversary of my coming out at work. There in the dark, all alone, I laughed—nothing was intentional about transitioning SEA Shell on that day. It just happened.

9 Life in a Corporate Diversity Center

For most of the next four years (November 1998 through August 2002), I was a consultant in the Shell Corporate Diversity Center, transcending the metamorphosis of the Diversity Center into a global practice as the U.S. operations for the Royal Dutch/Shell Group of companies evolved into global businesses. The full impact of changing careers hit me while I was carrying boxes from my office at the Westhollow Technology Center home instead of to my new office. I was literally putting my technical life in a closet while I followed my desire and interest in the field of diversity. It was quite a change trading a trailer office on the west side for an office in a downtown skyscraper with a panoramic view of west Houston.

The leadership of SEA Shell was something I missed dearly. Aside from one "on boarding" meeting with the new leadership, I rarely heard from SEA Shell. At times I felt like a castoff—they saw no value from my experience or the relationships I had nurtured over the years. Oh sure, I had friends in the network, but there was no role or process for leveraging someone with my experience in the new structure. I realized the new leaders had to establish themselves and a direction for the network without feeling they were operating in my shadow.

After winning domestic partner benefits, some GLBT networks lost momentum and struggled to find a purpose for existing. For SEA Shell the direction seemed clear—education and outreach. Among my successors were members of subcommittees interested in both areas and well qualified to guide the future direction of SEA Shell. Over time the network pulled together a module that could be used for short workshops or modified for lunch meetings to educate others on GLBT workplace issues. To give an idea of the reach of these efforts, in 2004, SEA Shell provided learning venues for about 1,000 employees. The facilitators were network members who were trained and volunteered their time to deliver the sessions.

The outreach efforts were twofold—external and internal to the company. External opportunities involved enhancing the visibility of Shell in the GLBT community and communicating Shell's efforts to create a more inclusive work environment to others. SEA Shell was also making recommendations for philanthropic giving in the community, some of which were included in the Shell Oil Company Foundation budget. Members of the network were also on a variety of boards and steering teams for non-profit organizations. They were ambassadors to the community. Internal to the company, SEA Shell pursued membership on many of the diversity councils and diversity action teams created by the various businesses. This was no small feat given there were around 30 councils and teams scattered across the company in the U.S. at the time.

SEA Shell had another internal challenge—the Alliance companies (Equilon, Motiva, and Equiva). These three companies were established to refine, distribute and market fuels in the U.S. SEA Shell, and the other Shell employee networks, had to cull out their employees in the Alliance companies. Because of the governance structure for the Alliance companies, their employees were no longer able to participate in the Shell employee networks—they had to form their own. Anyone who has been directly involved in creating an employee network knows the time, energy, sacrifices and patience invested by a few hard-working souls required to bring it all together. Each network leadership team took a hit in the culling process, as did each of the Executive Advisory Boards (EABs).

Having been instrumental in the construction of SEA Shell, I found myself in the position of "resident expert" on networks for the Corporate Diversity Center. This was an interesting situation, as I found myself at odds with my own beliefs. Personally, I didn't favor splitting the networks. GLBT employee networks tend to be small to start with. By reducing SEA Shell's numbers, I felt the network might lose traction at a crucial transition—they had just put their new leadership team in place.

From a company perspective I understood the reasons for the split, but that didn't prevent me from advocating positions I felt would assure the survival of SEA Shell. There was resistance from the networks to make the split, with most creating informal mechanisms for remaining somewhat connected. For example, SEA Shell steering team members were invited to attend the Alliance company GLBT network steering team meetings.

I was relieved that the Alliance companies had brought in Redia. Through our periodic meetings to become more acquainted, I had grown to know and trust her judgment. She was well versed in the value employee networks brought to the table. With Redia's support and guidance and the help of the Shell networks, the Alliance employee groups were quickly up and running. The GLBT group in the Alliance companies became Prism. Judy had agreed to be on the new advisory board for Prism and retain a relationship with the SEA Shell EAB.

Some in the Diversity Center seemed to value my insights about the networks, but it was pretty clear to me that sexual orientation and gender identity weren't going to get more attention because of my presence. Just because a company has a diversity center doesn't mean everyone in the center is GLBT friendly. The people in the Shell Diversity Center were an interesting mix—not just visibly, but also in backgrounds, thinking processes, and work styles. While the director was supportive of including sexual orientation as a facet of diversity, I would best assess the rest of my colleagues as being at various degrees of tolerance when it came to this topic, and generally unwilling to go there on issues pertaining to gender identity. Another way of looking at it—if the Diversity Center were a house and sexual orientation/gender identity were measures of how fit the house was to live in, I would say the Diversity Center was a reasonably-priced "fixer upper."

The company's definition of diversity was valuing all the ways we're different. Given the resources and the reality, one cannot work all facets of difference simultaneously. Strategic priorities were established and a framework developed that afforded the businesses the option of tailoring training toward their specific needs. For most the focus was on race and gender. Eventually some expanded awareness to difference in thinking, age, intercultural issues, etc. Very few tackled the topics of sexual orientation and gender identity as part of the formal training needs of the business. Since the idea of people being "committed" to diversity and inclusion was preferred to a "compliance" approach, diversity training wasn't mandatory for the businesses.

I reported to a team leader who reported to the diversity director. My team leader was a seasoned facilitator and coach with an HR background who, I think at the time, personally struggled with sexual orientation and gender identity. I was the first gay person brought into the Diversity Center. I brought a facet of diversity to the table that we as a team really weren't going to work, in spite of the definition of diversity. It took a couple of years and two more gay people on the team to finally bring him and others around.

My colleagues seemed okay with a gay person on the team as long as I worked the agenda around race and gender. I think there are a couple of reasons for this. Historically, race and gender have been the focus of programs like equal employment opportunity and Affirmative Action. As a result, some metrics were embedded in company HR systems and processes. When weighing risk and opportunities associated with diversity as a change management process, gender and race presented challenges to existing people systems that managers and HR professionals had some experience and history addressing.

The strategy for integrating diversity into the way the company conducted business involved meeting the businesses where they were on the topic, patiently coaching them to increase their awareness, and influencing them to be more progressive. For most of the businesses, the starting point was squarely in the arena of race and gender. Most of my colleagues in the Diversity Center were women and people of color who were well versed in these areas of difference.

A year after I entered the Diversity Center, some of my straight colleagues convinced the leadership that as a team we needed some training on the topics of sexual orientation and gender identity. I wrote the proposal and solicited different external consultants, and we ultimately settled on one. I think the daylong session helped people become more grounded in the subject matter. In some cases people began to see some of the barriers to inclusion. This didn't mean, however, that we as a team pursued the topic with more vigor in the businesses.

While team members knew I had a boyfriend, only a rare few would ask about him. I often attended holiday parties and other team outings alone because Slava was out of the country. Eventually I grew tired of going to events by myself and began declining all invitations unless Slava was in town to accompany me. I was determined to be true to myself in this new role, still sporting an earring—a fire opal set in a white-gold stud (Slava wears the other one)—which remained in my ear even when meeting with senior leaders.

My client groups were the IT business and the corporate firms (Tax, Finance, Legal, HR, Corporate Affairs, and Learning). My having more client groups than the other consultants was justified based on head count—the IT business and the firms comprised about 3,000 employees, comparable to the head counts of the other client group. I wasn't working directly with the employee base, but with the leadership teams and diversity councils for each client group. We were also expected to backfill for other consultants with their client groups, which happened on occasion.

While the opportunities broadened my learning, at times I also felt I was being set up to underperform and ultimately fail. Each of my peers had one client group. What they had to do once with their clients, I would have to repeat six times. The work environments for most of my clients felt far less tolerant than the Diversity Center.

For example, one of my first duties was meeting with the senior business leaders for each client group to assess their diversity journeys and understand the needs of each as seen through the eyes of the leaders. After the initial meeting, the diversity director asked whether my sexual orientation had come up in the dialogue. Being out of the scope of the meetings, it hadn't been a topic of conversation. She advised against approaching some of the leaders with the topic in the future, giving the impression that sexual orientation was a workplace issue they wouldn't tolerate.

Wanting to become established in the Diversity Center, I heeded her advice. I learned long ago that timing is everything when picking battles—the timing wasn't right to tackle conservative leaders whom I was just beginning to know. Initially I focused on establishing a baseline for these organizations around diversity and metrics for evaluating their progress.

The leader of the Learning organization felt diversity was well in hand, and as learning experts, his people were quite proficient on the topic. This was contrary to the message I had heard from others in his organization. The Learning organization was on the same floor as the Diversity Practice, so I would often see their leader in the hall. Each time I'd say hello; each time he'd walk by without a word or acknowledgement I even existed.

As bad as this may sound, it was still better then the leader of the IT business, who couldn't seem to find time for us to meet. I persistently scheduled and rescheduled meetings with him over a couple of months. Then one day I called his secretary to make yet another attempt. She replied, "It's pretty obvious to me he doesn't want to meet with you, so why don't you stop trying?" I was devastated, shocked, and most of all, pissed!

My bubble of optimism about choosing a career change was quickly deflating, and I'd only been in the job a few months. It was difficult for me to assess the drivers for these leaders' behavior—whether it was skepticism about my ability to bring value to their business, my sexual orientation, pre-occupation with other business priorities, or just being uninterested in the topic and wanting it to disappear.

I kept reinforcing myself to be the better man. Given the unfolding landscape, I had to make some tough personal decisions. To support this end I had to define my role—a painful process, given where my team leader was on the topic of sexual orientation. I am gay. Going back into a closet because I didn't conform to the personal values and beliefs of others was not an option. Sexual orientation was going to be on the table. At times this meant that I found myself operating outside of some of the team leader's directives.

A friend in the Diversity Center summed it up best when describing part of a conversation with our team leader, who at the time was irritated by my decision to skip a meeting he deemed important without first consulting with him. Afterward, I told my friend, "At times I believe it's better to beg forgiveness than ask permission." To which my friend replied, "Perhaps, but I've never seen you beg forgiveness."

Since leaving SEA Shell's leadership, I was "searching for my soul." The void left had to be filled, so I made a conscious decision to strengthen my position as a thought leader on GLBT workplace issues. The implication was that people would seek my advice and counsel, thus I would become a noted subject matter expert. Shell would have to decide whether to leverage or suppress my interest in being a thought leader.

Fortunately, I still had Richard—although his health continued to deteriorate, he remained very active as a mentor. When the Diversity Center created a Community Advisory panel to act as a sounding board for Shell's strategy on workplace diversity, I suggested perhaps a GLBT community representative might be appropriate. The GLBT Chamber of Commerce seemed to be a viable place to look, so an invitation was extended, and as vice president of the Chamber, Richard accepted.

Richard found himself meeting people he had only previously been able to picture through our conversations. He was a very effective communicator and engaged the diversity director on several occasions about positioning of GLBT workplace issues. I think the experience also helped him apply a more focused approach to my development needs. As opportunities presented themselves, he encouraged their pursuit, and there were plenty to choose from.

Through an exchange of e-mails, Ronnie pondered whether I'd still be supportive of him and transgender workplace issues. I assured him that being supportive and staying in the learning process was still important. As part of the dialogue, he made me aware of the Unity Banquet, a formal gathering of the transgender community to recognize their accomplishments for the year.

The first one I attended was at an Italian restaurant on the west side of town. I felt a little uncomfortable at first, but everyone was so friendly and welcoming that I quickly felt quite at home. I enjoyed the evening, met some great people, and learned from some of the community leaders about the legal and political struggles of their niche of the GLBT community.

Members of SEA Shell were still struggling with how to embrace gender identity as part of their mission—the Unity Banquet was certainly a good starting point to broaden their understanding of the community. I had suggested to Ronnie that he share the opportunity with others on the steering team and try to influence some of them to attend in the future.

When the HRC Business Council initiated the process of selecting a new co-chair, I found myself the front-runner. Richard was very supportive. Rather than ask permission, I chose to accept the role and responsibilities, and then tell my team leader of the appointment. If I had asked permission, I was certain he would have wanted me to decline the opportunity. This was evidenced a couple of years later when the co-chair role was up for renewal—one option was for me to serve a second term. I approached my team leader with the idea, which he discouraged.

The position was aligned with my development needs and aspirations of becoming a thought leader. The role required dedicating a significant chunk of time to Business Council activities, bringing added responsibility. I was apprehensive about whether I was up to the task. This was an important role—I'd be co-chairing with Louise from Raytheon and working more closely with Daryl, both of whom I admired greatly and considered far more versed in leadership and strategy then I. They were great coaches —I was quickly on boarded and immersed in the ongoing operations of leading the team.

Equally important was the support of other Business Council members. During my two years as co-chair we promoted more visibility for the Business Council within HRC through board presentations, visibility at various functions, and increasing the number of endorsements of the Employment Non-Discrimination Act (ENDA). Externally we promoted education and awareness of GLBT workplace issues at various conferences.

A year into the position, I found myself filling Louise's shoes as I mentored and on boarded her successor, Ellen. Louise was a tough act to follow, but I did my best helping Ellen learn the ropes. As Louise had positioned me front and center during the twilight of our duet, I did the same with Ellen before stepping down from my role as chair.

There was no shortage of things to do socially—Richard and his partner, Ian, and a lesbian couple, Vickie and Clyde, had decided to formalize their relationships with commitment ceremonies. Richard and Ian asked that I give a formal toast at their reception for their spring ceremony. I tried not to worry about Richard, but it was hard. He was becoming so fragile and had been sick just prior to the ceremony. Ian had been by his side all the time, caring for him. In spite of his health, everything finally came together for the waterfront ceremony in League City, and we all toasted the happy couple. Slava had met Richard and Ian on a number of occasions. He knew the place Richard held in my heart. While he couldn't be at the ceremony, Slava forwarded his best wishes to Ian and Richard.

Vickie and Clyde had other revelations. They had attended Richard and Ian's ceremony. Seeing me give the toast was enough for them to decide I'd be ideal for presiding over their ceremony. I had met Clyde, a prominent Houston defense attorney, through the board position with the Greater Houston GLBT Chamber of Commerce. Her partner, Vickie, worked for Shell Chemical—we had met while I was a leader in SEA Shell.

They assured me it would be a small event with just family and close friends. I accepted the offer, later discovering that family and close friends accounted for about 500 people in a ballroom at a downtown hotel in Houston. In addition to leaders from the GLBT community and the city, there were also a number of people from Shell.

The way the program was choreographed, I was the first person entering the ballroom to greet everyone and kick off the ceremony. Fortunately the brides had created a script for the entire event. While I knew most of the lines, I had the book with me, just in case. In the jacket pocket of my tuxedo was a picture—as in the past, when I found myself in front of a large crowd and Slava wasn't in the sea of people, I put a picture of him next to my heart.

It didn't help that we started the ceremony late; I was already nervous enough. Taking a deep breath, I walked into the ballroom, eyes forward, took the stage, and pivoted to address the audience. I could tell my voice was shaking when I blurted out the welcome message and apologized for the delay. There was no turning back —like it or not, the show was going forward.

I had a few moments while the rest of the procession came up on the stage. Most of those moments were spent searching my mind for some peaceful moment I could dwell upon to calm myself. Unfortunately, nothing was coming to mind. Then the brides began their procession down the aisle with a lone bagpiper leading the way. It was the music from the bagpipes that soothed my nerves.

I'm not an ordained minister, and this wasn't a wedding. However, I am one who knows the importance of the ties that bind a relationship between two people who sacrifice everything for each other as an act of love. It was not in my power to marry them, but one day I hope they have that opportunity. I saw no less joy or nervousness, and just as many tears of happiness as I've seen at countless weddings for heterosexuals.

During preparations for the ceremony, Vickie and Clyde struggled to get the announcement of their union in the *Houston Chronicle*, having gone down to the *Chronicle* offices and met with people from the bridal section of the paper. With a little handholding, the newspaper had agreed to publish the announcement of their union. After the announcement came out in the paper, friends had sent copies to my office. They were surprised by my officiating the ceremony. I reminded them the union was symbolic and had no meaning in the eyes of the law.

More interesting was the reaction of some of my diversity colleagues asking what Shell thought of the article (Vickie had referenced Shell as her employer). My response was, "Who cares?" After all, had this been a wedding announcement for a heterosexual Shell employee, no one would have batted an eyelash. I was honored to have the opportunity to officiate their ceremony.

As a co-chair for the HRC Business Council, I was also periodically called upon to promote efforts to create a more inclusive workplace. While attending the Society of Human Resource Managers (SHRM) conference in Washington, D.C., I decided to spend the first morning staffing the HRC booth. The advantage for HRC was having someone from corporate America in the both to share his experiences with people from other businesses wrestling with GLBT workplace issues. For me it was an opportunity to network with others in various companies wanting to understand and work the issues.

I had fun talking with HR managers and professionals from other companies about GLBT workplace topics. It was no surprise that many were looking for resources to help them position GLBT topics for discussion with leaders in their companies. They seemed pleasantly surprised to find a Shell diversity professional helping with the HRC booth. The partnership with HRC at the event furthered their credibility as a workplace resource. People were picking up as much material as they could carry.

The following week I was in Atlanta as part of a HRC Business Council panel for the Out & Equal Workplace conference, talking about "Working with Company Leadership." Public speaking isn't something that comes easily for me—I have to talk myself into it. I agreed to participate on the panel because I needed the experience, the exposure, and the practice. Basically, the only way to get good at something is to practice, and the experience prepared me for future engagements.

Knowing where the team dynamics were on the topic at work, I didn't ask my team leader whether I could participate in functions supporting HRC efforts around workplace advocacy. My sense was that if I asked, he'd find "more important" things requiring my attention. I wasn't giving him the benefit of the doubt. I knew sexual orientation and gender identity couldn't dominate the agenda of a Diversity Center, but had the center been more inclusive of these topics when I arrived, I'd have been more open about the opportunities I was pursuing. When I first arrived in the Diversity Center, I had the perception that my GLBT community activities were viewed as something in addition to my regular workload as a diversity consultant. The added burden of GLBT workplace issues wasn't even a variable for my overall performance evaluation.

With my growing exposure to GLBT workplace advocacy, Richard was anxious for me to write a book. After I'd spent several years out in the workplace, he felt some great lessons should be captured and published about creating employee networks, working with leaders, obtaining domestic partner benefits, and my development as a thought leader on GLBT workplace issues. As we began crafting an outline, I was looking for something more—beyond forming networks and domestic partner benefits, what were the drivers for the continuing viability of these groups? There just seemed to be something missing that I couldn't quite put my finger on.

Around this time a storm began brewing in corporate America. Exxon announced the acquisition of Mobil Corporation—a merger that brought together the two largest pieces of the old Standard Oil trust of John D. Rockefeller. The new company, ExxonMobil, was the largest integrated oil company in the world. With the acquisition, Exxon eliminated all of Mobil's GLBT supportive workplace policies—removing sexual orientation from the company nondiscrimination policy and discontinuing the offering of domestic partner benefits to anyone not already enrolled.

The policy change created a huge uproar in the GLBT community. In spite of the opposition, the leadership of ExxonMobil remained firm in their position. Being in Houston, and in an energy company, I found myself being sucked into the fracas. A couple of organizations had asked if I would participate in meetings with some of the ExxonMobil senior leaders, but I respectfully declined.

As a Shell employee I was concerned there might be some confusion about my representation or role while in a meeting with ExxonMobil managers. So I decided to test the situation with a couple of people. In separate conversations I explained the situation to the Shell diversity director and Redia, the diversity director for the Alliance companies. Redia suggested I attend the meetings and clarify my role up front with the participants. The Shell diversity director, however, strongly supported the opposing view. Personally, I agreed with Redia, but had to succumb to the reality of who I worked for and his position. I didn't like being on the sidelines, but because of a desire by others for me to be transparent on the issue, that's exactly where I found myself—invisible.

However, I did choose to be active in other ways, providing advice on strategy, being a resource on GLBT-friendly policies among other oil and gas companies, and participating in the protests. All these were things I could do on my own time. The Houston Activist Network (HAN-Net), an online Yahoo group for Houston's GLBT activists, was a phenomenal resource documenting the various efforts underway to persuade ExxonMobil to reconsider. It was through HAN-Net that much of the information on the protest marches in Houston was coordinated. HRC was instrumental in coordinating a national outcry from the GLBT community and its allies, resulting in tens of thousands of e-mails and messages flooding the Irvine, Texas, headquarters of ExxonMobil.

I can still remember that cold, windy, drizzly afternoon when about a hundred protesters gathered in a downtown park before marching on the Exxon building. As ill as he was, Richard wanted to march, and I stayed by him through the entire event. I wasn't sure he'd be able to withstand the cold, but he mustered his strength from somewhere and stuck it out.

Later I discovered from friends at ExxonMobil that the company had actually sent employees in the downtown office building home early. It makes me wonder about the business thinking of the leadership—what they lost that afternoon in productivity would probably have covered the costs of maintaining the benefits and policy changes instituted by Mobil.

In the spring of 2000 a shareholder resolution was submitted for vote on including sexual orientation in the ExxonMobil nondiscrimination policy. That year the resolution gained a few percent of stockholders in favor of the change. Each year since, the resolution continues to come up for a vote, and each year management has refused to change the policy. In 2007 the shareholder resolution had the support of about 35% of the stock being voted, yet Exxon still refuses to change the policy.

With the arrival of warm spring weather also came devastating news—late on the evening of April 28th, 2000, I was packing to catch a flight to Washington, D.C., for the Millennium March. The purpose of the march was to promote equality for the GLBT community and was expected to draw about a million people. Richard had attended the first march on Washington decades prior, which had a profound influence on shaping his role as a community activist. He really encouraged my participation in the march, as it might be years before another opportunity would arise.

Late in the evening as I was packing, Ian called to tell me Richard had died. He had hung on long enough for his sister to drive up from Kemah and his daughter to arrive from Dallas. Then with a smile and a wink of an eye, he passed away.

I fell to the floor, not believing what I was hearing. It was just a bad dream, and I'd awake to find everything was fine. That wasn't the case. I told Ian I'd cancel the trip to be with him, but he insisted I go. Richard was excited I was going to be part of the Millennium March, and he'd have wanted me to go. I called Slava the next morning—he too was devastated by the news. Richard had always treated Slava with the same respect and affection he bestowed on me. We were both sobbing over the loss, and I agreed to call him when I knew the details for the funeral.

I flew to Washington, D.C., tears streaming down my face most of the way, and participated in the Millennium March. The event was so surreal; I just wandered aimlessly in an ocean of people awash with the colors of the rainbow. There were so many marchers there, some of whom knew Richard. Because they had been in D.C. for a few days, they had not heard that Richard had passed away. I chose not to tell them—the Millennium March was all about celebrating pride, and I didn't want to place a somber cloud over the event for others from Houston.

The memorial service for Richard was a couple of weeks later in May. I went alone; Slava was unable to get the time off work. This was to have been Richard's year—just before passing he was selected to be a grand marshal for the Houston Gay Pride parade. Richard was excited about riding in the parade with his partner, daughter and grandson.

The memorial tribute to Richard was very fitting. It was held at the Brownstone, one of Richard's favorite restaurants. Ian and Karie had asked me to offer Richard one last toast. When the champagne was poured, I had arranged for three Lalique angel-wing flutes to be filled—two were gifts for Ian and Karie, and the third would be mine. Richard had been an angel to so many, the flutes seemed a befitting memento of his life.

I've never quite gotten over the loss of Richard. To this day I still draw upon him for inspiration and occasionally, courage. A few days after the memorial service, I stopped by the house to see Ian—he had a few things he thought Richard would want me to have back. Among them was the outline for a book. Ian shared that Richard had thought it was great—his one desire was for me to get on with the writing, something I seemed to have trouble finding time to do.

I was struggling with the loss of my mentor. All these years Richard had believed in me—now I had to believe in myself. A few months after his death I found myself in a GLBT Executive Leadership course at UCLA. During one of the sessions we touched on the role of mentors and renegotiating the relationships as one becomes more senior in the leadership of an organization. After class I asked the instructor if she had any insights regarding the loss of a mentor. I shared the story of Richard's passing and expressed my frustration of feeling analogous to a half-baked pizza.

She listened intently, suggesting the time might be right for me to begin mentoring others. Her observation was based on the premise of having just as much to learn from the "mentee" as I had to give. Taking her advice, I began opening myself up for others to learn from, giving career advice, insights on the development of other networks, and suggestions to help others engage leaders. Ultimately no one ever replaced Richard or filled his shoes. Yet I have continued to learn and grow through helping others and seeing different experiences through their eyes.

Back in the office, I began searching for situations lending themselves to inclusion of learning components on sexual orientation and gender identity. Each year the Diversity Center would host an internal Diversity Conference to share best practices across businesses and expose change agents to new skills and competencies. Each year I made an effort to ensure that there would be at least one workshop on sexual orientation.

During the third conference I was asked advice on possible keynotes. Usually the keynote was someone external to Shell who represented an organization considered to be a leader in some facet of diversity—my suggestion was Elizabeth Birch. At the time, Elizabeth Birch was the leader of the Human Rights Campaign, a large, well-respected, non-government organization (NGO) pursuing basic rights for GLBT Americans.

The conference team proposed the idea—our team leader vetoed the choice—his boss overrode the veto. I was very excited about having Elizabeth come to speak. I worked closely with her secretary to develop a sense of the direction for her remarks. Since the CEO was going to introduce her, I thought it best for them and any other Shell leaders available to meet over breakfast before the conference. This marked the first time a representative of the GLBT civil rights movement would speak to a large audience of Shell employees and leaders.

I didn't see Elizabeth's introduction by the CEO or hear her words that day. Three weeks prior to the event I suffered another major setback—after coming home from a long workday, I sat down to watch the evening news. As Dan Rather began his narrative for the evening, I felt heaviness building in my chest, followed by the onset of numbness in my arm and a clammy sweat. I knew what these symptoms might mean—heart issues had plagued my family for generations. I took two aspirin and lay on the couch for a few minutes to see if the symptoms would ease—they did.

While the sweating and the numbness had dissipated, the chest pain was still very intense. I got off the couch and drove myself to a nearby hospital. The emergency room made me a priority. While there were no blood enzymes indicating a heart attack, they thought it prudent to keep me overnight for observation given that my blood pressure was through the roof. They called my team leader, leaving a message that I wasn't coming in for work the next day. In the early hours of the morning I had a massive heart attack. Later in the morning Dr. Miller introduced himself and explained my condition—basically, three blocked arteries. He was the doctor on call that night and was responsible for my still being alive.

That afternoon my team leader dropped by the ICU—he had just gotten the message. He shared an update with others in the Diversity Center about my condition. A friend also came by that day asking if Slava knew what had happened. Slava had just gone back to Europe about three weeks prior. I really didn't want him to worry. So I asked my friend to give him a call, tell him that I was okay and going to be fine, and not to worry about feeling like he had to come back over.

I was concerned that Slava wouldn't be able to get back into the country—he had spent about as much time as legally possible in the U.S. already. I didn't want him to feel bad or in some way responsible if he was denied re-entry. The message I had relayed via a friend was an attempt on my part to dispel any regrets he might feel if he couldn't come back into the U.S.

After my friend relayed the message, Slava asked him, "What do you think I should do?" To which our friend replied, "Get the hell on a plane and get back over here!" Unbeknownst to me, Slava got a ticket, and he came back for another two months. I found out when he walked into my hospital room. For the next month I was in and out of the hospital and home recovering. I couldn't have managed without him. Had he not been there I would have spent more days in the hospital because there would not have been someone at home to care for me.

At the time of Elizabeth's speech, I was home recovering between hospital visits. I wanted so much to be there, but that just wasn't going to happen. Mid-morning the phone rang—someone was yelling something over the noise of a crowd. A friend attending the conference called to tell me that Elizabeth's speech was a big hit and there was someone who wanted to talk to me. The next voice I heard was Elizabeth's. She asked how I was feeling and recommended getting plenty of rest. Maybe I was there after all. Although I was not in the room, I knew people were thinking about me, a huge morale boost at a moment in my life when I was feeling helpless and weak.

By early October I was back at work. There were about 2,000 e-mails in my inbox, my voicemail was full, and all my projects were exactly where I had left them. The e-mails and the voicemails I had expected, but the projects were a big surprise. Prior to my heart attack these were high priorities; deadlines had to be met and things had to keep moving. To come back and find them exactly where I had left them gave pause for thought about the true priorities of the Diversity Center and the perceived value of my contributions.

My team leader's explanation was that I knew the projects best and there were no resources to backfill in my absence, so a decision was made not to progress with them. The explanation didn't help—after a life-threatening experience, one has a tendency to view each day and each task differently. In my mind these projects, which had been sapping both my time and energy, ultimately were a low priority and of little worth.

There were plans later that month for a Global Shell Diversity Practice conference in Barcelona, Spain, with virtually all the staff attending. Again my team leader came into my office to say that because of my absence, there were reservations about whether I should be attending the conference. If I was going, I was expected to make a presentation. To my knowledge, presenting was not a pre-requisite for anyone else. It bothered me to suddenly be in a position of having to justify my worth and value to the organization. I took in the conversation and agreed to a presentation—since my projects hadn't progressed, I just dusted off a slide pack from before the heart attack.

Life in the office after returning from medical leave really made me rethink how best to invest my time and energy. I decided it was time to move on, dusting off my resume and defining in my mind what the next assignment should look like. As I thought it through, I wanted the next position to be a promotion allowing me to build on my skills and competencies as an environmental and diversity professional.

A few months later, during my annual performance review, I shared my desire to move on. My team leader seemed eager to support my efforts, coming into my office weekly thereafter to evaluate my progress. This was really annoying and not very conducive to enhancing my productivity while I was still a diversity consultant. So one day when he asked, I cut him short—making quite clear I would leave when the next logical opportunity for the progression of my career became available. I don't think he cared for the answer.

What I couldn't understand was whether his attitude was being driven by my medical condition, my sexual orientation, some combination of both, or something else. My performance evaluations had been very good, my clients seemed very satisfied with my work—so it wasn't a matter of my ability to do the job.

Whether real or perceived, the experience made me acutely aware of my own vulnerabilities. I viewed my sexual orientation (and to a lesser extent, my health) as career limiting—rationalizing that if these issues were coming up for me, they were probably also on the minds on my superiors in their decision-making about staffing and assignments—paranoia perhaps, but my reality nonetheless. The behavior of my supervisor certainly reinforced these perceptions.

I was determined not to go back in the closet. So in posting for a new position, I made clear during the interview process my sexual orientation. If I could not advance being openly gay, then the system was failing me and needed more work rather than some thought.

Slava really struggled with what I was doing for a living. Being European, he was working from a different cultural background and applied different mental models when thinking about diversity and inclusion. In his mind, laws were in place to ensure people fair opportunity in employment and housing. To give Slava a better sense of what I was doing, we signed up for a White Male Caucus offered by a consulting team, "White Men as Full Diversity Partners." I had experienced the caucus concept as part of a strategy I had developed for engaging white men in diversity at Shell. Basically, the caucus provided the opportunity for white males to come together and talk about themselves as a "culture," explore the issues of power and privilege, racism, sexism, and heterosexism, and identify where they were individually in their learning journeys.

Slava and I flew to Portland, Oregon, made the drive to Glenwood, Washington, and settled in for three days of intense learning in the shadows of Mt. Adams. Two things happened during the caucus. One, Slava gained a much different perspective of U.S.

white males and their culture. Two, the other participants had a real conversation with a gay couple about life in a world that doesn't recognize our relationship.

For the first time Slava knew what I did for a living and why the work was so important. Even he admitted that the session had opened his eyes to things he hadn't considered in his interactions with women and people of color. For others in the class, they heard about immigration issues, travel costs, trying to take care of each other when we lived on different continents, etc.

Slava supported my decisions about my career. With each new assignment I hoped for more travel to Europe to ease the strain of the distance in our relationship. Each new assignment brought virtually nothing in the way of relief. So Slava and I made the best of my three weeks of vacation and the time off he could take to nurture our relationship.

- We all have some learning to do, including myself. Just because a company has a Diversity Center doesn't mean inclusion of sexual orientation and gender identity is a given. When it comes to understanding risks and embracing opportunities associated with change, Diversity Centers are staffed by people with some of the same shortcomings as everyone else.

- Having a GLBT employee network doesn't guarantee inclusion of gender identity as a given. The gay and lesbian workplace community at times struggles with the issue of gender identity and in some cases even bisexuality.

- Employee networks can be extremely effective vehicles for outreach and education about workplace issues. After domestic partner benefits, SEA Shell moved toward addressing these tough issues.

- Growth and development as a thought leader meant taking the reins of my career. While still working within the systems and processes of the company, I made a conscious effort to make time and space among all the other priorities for my own professional needs.

- Slava and I worked very hard at making our relationship work. It took a tremendous investment of time and energy to maintain, which was more of a priority to me than the Diversity Center.
- I tend to be most productive when motivated by the people I work with. The challenges of the diversity assignment were taxing, and the environment was not the most stimulating.
- I made a conscious effort to find my identity after SEA Shell. My work responsibilities didn't afford much in the way of development as a thought leader on GLBT issues. So I deliberately sought opportunities, sometimes to the chagrin of my leadership, to assure parts of my identity weren't completely suppressed, forcing me back to a life in the closet.
- The loss of my mentor and friend, Richard, was very troubling—there was no transition or closure for me from the loss. I had to pull the pieces together and move on, remembering his words and lessons. He had taken me far enough—I could mentor others and still do so today.
- I learned to meet business leaders where they were in their personal learning process. At times they could be disrespectful, and I made a conscious effort not to mimic that facet of their behavior. I treated them with dignity and respect, even when they showed little to me.
- After a life-threatening experience, priorities change. I learned to assess the perceived sense of urgency others placed on projects. I also felt a sense of diminished value

to the organization from the behavior of leadership after I returned to the workplace. Not just words, but even the actions and behaviors of leaders send messages.

10 Influencing Change at the Top

By the summer of 1999 there was another leadership change—Steve Miller assumed the roles of chairman and CEO for Shell Oil Company. A career Shell employee, rising through the ranks of the oil products business, Steve had been a member of the Committee of Managing Directors (CMD) for the Royal Dutch/Shell Group—the third American to hold such an honor in the century-old company. I really didn't know Steve. He and I had both "grown up" in the same part of the business, but he had transferred to Europe before I reached Shell's corporate offices in Houston.

My first opportunity to meet Steve occurred at a reception welcoming him back to the U.S. It was a very pleasant event at the Plaza Club high atop One Shell Plaza. After an hour or so of mingling, I saw Steve at a table with a manager I knew from the Exploration & Production side of the business. Drumming up a little courage, I decided to go join them. A conversation ensued and I discovered Steve had a genuine interest in leadership, which turned out to be the starting point upon which we could build a working relationship.

With our initial conversation came my first lesson—leaders tend to do their best learning when they step out of their comfort zone. Well, sitting down at a table with the new CEO of Shell Oil Company was way out of my comfort zone. Steve was a gracious host, and I think he saw that my interest in leadership was sincere.

As the conversation ended, he offered to forward some references I might find helpful. Within a couple of days they were on my desk.

A few weeks later, while going through the latest issue of *Fast Company*, I came across an insert on leadership. The special section was profiling key thoughts from 10 corporate leaders. As I flipped through the section, soaking up the words of wisdom, I couldn't help but think, wouldn't it be great if someday Shell had a leader that would be profiled in this context? When I flipped the page to see the 7th leader profile—it was Steve. I was very pleasantly surprised and quickly sent a short e-mail off to Steve congratulating him on being a part of a great article.

Steve replied back later in thc day. As busy as he was, he had found time to reply to my e-mail. This was good to know, and I was careful not to abuse the knowledge. I knew there were going to be times when I would need to send things to Steve, and I wanted my notes to be few and important rather than many and benign. Building credibility and trust with leaders was an important first step in my mind.

With Steve's appointment as CEO of Shell Oil Company came a number of other announcements about changes at the top. Shortly thereafter an announcement came down that the corporate diversity director would be assuming the role of global diversity leader for Royal Dutch/Shell and relocating to London. In the new role she would be accountable to the chairman, Sir Mark Moody-Stuart, and the head of the global HR function. The Diversity Center would become part of a global Diversity Practice, which would include other offices in London and Kuala Lumpur. This change supported my belief that diversity was here to stay—after all, why implement a global strategy for diversity if the company wasn't in it for the long haul?

The diversity director's replacement heading up U.S. operations was the leader of the Learning Group, one of my clients. I greeted this part of the announcement with a great deal of skepticism. I aired my reservations over the new appointment. In my time working with the Learning Group, I had found the leadership to be anything but supportive of diversity.

The diversity director suggested I try to bundle up my frustrations and set them aside to create a clean slate—asking that I give Steve Miller a chance to get settled and set a direction that would in part define the role of the new diversity leader in the U.S. Reluctantly I agreed to reserve judgment and to store my "baggage" on the appointment. In return, she would suggest that her replacement schedule meetings with the Diversity Practice to share his background and thoughts on why he was the right guy for the job.

The new diversity leader agreed to the meetings, and I was front and center for the first one. He spent about 30 minutes providing an overview of his background and why he felt suited to replace the diversity director as a focal point in the U.S. reporting to the CEO. To his credit, I knew he could be effective and tactful influencing organizational change. After his comments the new diversity leader offered to take questions from the Diversity Practice members in the room. There was silence.

As I looked around the room, no one appeared ready to say anything. So I took the leap, making the observation that past experience working with him and the Learning Group had showed me no evidence of his support for diversity. I further added that this was my "baggage," I had to deal with it, and I was willing to shelve it and start from a clean slate. My real question was, what had changed that should give me confidence in his leadership? Before he could answer, my team leader quickly intervened by acknowledging my courage to bring up a tough issue that was on the minds of others.

Replying to the question, the new diversity leader acknowledged his indifference to diversity in the past. He offered that in this new role he was accountable for diversity in Shell U.S. and would work diligently to maintain progress, asking that I give him the chance to demonstrate his level of commitment. He could have skirted the question in any number of ways, but chose to tackle the issue head on. I have always admired honesty and respected those who acknowledge ownership of their past. Hearing the diversity leader's words and believing what he said to be true was integral to my giving him my support.

I was not disappointed—the new diversity leader went on to be highly effective in promoting diversity in Shell. His interests in diversity were very inclusive, going beyond race and gender to include other tough topics, ranging from sexual orientation and gender identity to engaging white males as full diversity partners. I expected nothing less than tangible proof and received nothing less.

Other changes occurred after Steve became CEO—the "old guard" in the corporate firms chose to retire. The new face for HR was from the outside, David, a retired general who was the Army's equivalent to a vice president of HR. David had been with the Pentagon during the Clinton administration and the creation of "don't ask, don't tell"—the military's answer to addressing GLBT people in the service.

"Don't ask, don't tell" basically means the military would no longer ask a soldier about his or her sexual orientation, and as long as a soldier wasn't out, the military wouldn't discharge him or her. In the event a soldier self-identified as homosexual, the military would grant an honorable discharge. The U.S. military still has a way to go on the topic when compared with our allies around the world, some of which allow GLBT troops to serve openly and honorably.

At some point I wanted to explore the thinking behind "don't ask, don't tell" with David, but not during our first encounter. Our first meeting provided some impressionable insights—a West Point graduate, David was every bit a leader, and I was left with an appreciation for his rise to the rank of general.

It was during David's watch that the Boy Scouts of America (BSA) made clear their intent to expel any gay scouts or scout masters discovered in the organization. Their actions caused a number of businesses to reassess whether to maintain ties with BSA. The controversy led to some United Way chapters and corporations pulling their support for BSA. Even various troops of the BSA questioned and were reluctant to enforce the policy. Those troops not enforcing the divisive policy were threatened with losing their charter.

Many in the GLBT community were hot over the issue—those in the Houston Activists Network (HAN-Net) were bristling. The GLBT community had not singled out Shell for action, but the community had recognized that Shell leaders were on some of the boards locally. Companies with leaders holding board positions with BSA were logical first targets to be approached, and Shell could possibly be asked to clarify their position.

My involvement was as a subject matter expert summarizing the facts. Every day I'd peruse the web, assessing how the community, businesses, and United Way were reacting to the BSA position on homosexuality. I would prepare a short assessment for my team leader, who would share it with others in leadership. While this was not something he asked for, I thought they might be helpful in some way.

Eventually I was asked to brief David, giving him an overview of the situation and some possible alternatives. The ideal outcome in my mind would have been for Shell to cut all ties to the BSA—one alternative I proposed. Another would have been to do nothing, but given the associations some senior leaders had with the BSA, this would have been an unsustainable position.

There was some middle ground. Other Houston-based corporations weren't interested in the BSA issue. GLBT employees in other companies were either not raising the issue or were unsuccessful in influencing their business leaders to take a stand. Not surprising, since the BSA has a longstanding reputation of developing future leaders. My experience is that if the troops won't rally around the cause, the campaign fails.

I was searching for the high ground—in my mind energy and resources were best utilized influencing United Way to broaden their portfolio to include organizations that welcomed at risk GLBT youth and offered them development opportunities denied by the BSA. This was the middle ground I pursued with David, and I suggested the employee networks might be of help.

I found David was not one to shy away from tough issues—with Steve's support, he and leaders from Corporate Affairs partnered with the employee networks to take up the task of developing a position for Shell. While not the ideal resolution, the recommendation was for United Way to review its funding distribution, encouraging inclusion of organizations that offered support to GLBT youth alienated by BSA because of their sexual orientation.

Not all scouting troops, even in Houston, agreed with BSA. An employee of Shell who was also active with a local scouting troop during these events gave me a call wanting to explore what their troop could do to be more supportive. Given the national BSA position on homosexuality, the local troop had decided to adopt a "don't ask, don't tell" strategy. They were not about to deny any youth the opportunity to be a scout—a position taken by other troops in the country.

During a follow-up conversation with David, I took the opportunity to pursue my curiosity about "don't ask, don't tell." To the extent he could share, I wanted to understand some of the thinking and rationale leading up to the policy change. David shared some of his thoughts. My take on the conversation was that the Army tries to stay in step with society when making policy decisions. As U.S. society progresses on the issues, so does the Army. "Don't ask, don't tell" seemed to be in step with where society's thinking was at that time. He felt as society moved to be more inclusive, so would the military. For instance, passage of a bill like ENDA could influence the U.S. military to reassess their policy.

Other new faces appeared among my clients. Pat assumed the leadership role for the tax organization, and Cathy became general counsel for Shell Oil Company. Diversity and inclusion finally began to take root in these organizations under their leadership.

Pat replaced his predecessor on the SEA Shell Executive Advisory Board. While no longer a leader for SEA Shell, Pat would periodically canvass my thoughts and advice. I tried to be as objective as possible by sharing the potential benefits and weighing the possible risks. When discussing risks, I also provided suggestions for their mitigation. Over time Pat became a very supportive ally, realizing diversity and inclusion was about treating people the way they wanted to be treated.

Cathy and I had met a few years prior in my career at a service anniversary dinner for an old friend working for her in the legal department. I found Cathy to be very approachable and had a very good impression of her. Under her leadership, diversity and inclusion thrived in the Legal organization. She integrated accountability for diversity in the daily business of the firm and established a key performance indicator to assure measurement of progress.

Overall, I thought Steve made some remarkable choices in the leadership for Shell in the U.S. In his role Steve provided visionary leadership and a framework within which the businesses could operate effectively. To achieve this directive, he created the "Blueprint for Success," a concise document laying out the values and general business directives of Shell and the key planks for achieving success, among them a commitment to diversity and inclusion.

When it came to supporting these new leaders on sexual orientation as a workplace issue, my role with the HRC Business Council and being positioned in the Shell Diversity Practice established my credibility as a resource. I had also retained membership with the Greater Houston GLBT Chamber of Commerce, which was invaluable as a networking resource.

I relied on the HAN-Net online message board for the real time information on what was pressing to the GLBT community on a day-by-day basis. Every morning I'd get a cup of coffee, log in and review the traffic on HAN-Net. Rarely would I reply, only wanting the pulse of the community. Ironically, about the time I left the Shell Diversity Practice, the owner of HAN-NET decided to shut the group down. He thought it was a very helpful tool and it had offered a great forum for the community, but he wanted to retire the group and move on to other things.

My close ties and reputation with the Media Relations group in External Affairs added to my credibility as a thought leader. I was often sought to provide talking points and responses to questions from reporters on Shell's policies affecting GLBT employees. A writer might also call the HRC soliciting information for a story and the HRC might refer them to me for a response. Being on the HRC Business Council provided many of these opportunities. All of these calls were important to me because they provided another venue for getting the word out on the work Shell was doing.

Sometimes the replies required partnering with the appropriate people in HR to craft responses for inquiries from Media Relations. They rarely changed anything I wrote. The relationships cultivated over the years were very helpful in getting the word out about Shell's progressive workplace policies.

Of course, getting the word out also meant getting some backlash, and I learned to prepare for those occasions. There were the occasional letters and cut-up credit cards from disgruntled customers who saw Shell's policies of promoting inclusion as an assault on their personal values. Sometimes these letters went to the CEO, and I would be asked to take a shot at crafting a response. The first time I drafted a response, I was very apologetic. The draft was considered completely unacceptable and I was directed to try again. On my next attempt I promoted the company's interest in diversity and inclusion as a business imperative, respectfully disagreed with the customer's views, and hoped they would reconsider. This time the letter went through with modest edits.

Helping with these responses drove home a couple of points for me: 1) It was important to have a meaningful business case for inclusion of sexual orientation and gender identity in the diversity efforts of a company; and 2) This wasn't about personal values—it was about expected behaviors and treating people with dignity and respect.

Not all the work I did with Steve was in defense of sexual orientation and gender identity. There were other occasions when I was asked to provide information in support of social policy change at the local, state and national level. Among these efforts, Steve supported the city of Houston's adding sexual orientation and gender identity to their nondiscrimination policy, opposed a referendum on the ballot that would prevent the city from extending domestic partner benefits to eligible employees, supported the James Byrd Hate Crimes Act, and endorsed ENDA.

I felt a part of my role was to bring opportunities to Shell's attention. I raised them first with my team leader and the U.S. diversity leader. They would raise them with Steve, and I would be directed to craft the appropriate supporting materials (e.g. white papers, talking points, letters, etc.). Throughout this process it was very clear to me that Steve was becoming comfortable with inclusion of GLBT issues in the definition of diversity.

I wasn't the only one helping with Steve's learning—the networks were also supporting his education. Shortly after taking the CEO job, Steve arranged to meet quarterly with the leadership teams from each of the employee networks, including SEA Shell. It was through these exchanges that Steve was able to more readily connect with the grassroots portion of the organization. In essence, they helped him build a broader foundation supporting some of his decision-making and learning.

When I heard Steve was going to be meeting with the leadership of each of the employee networks, my primary concern was Sara. To my knowledge, Steve had not met someone who was transgender before. I was worried about the meeting being awkward. When I shared my concerns with some of my colleagues, they seemed confident Steve could handle the situation. In response I told them it wasn't Steve I was worried about—I didn't want the situation to be awkward for Sara.

My concerns were forwarded. The day of the SEA Shell meeting with Steve, Sara was running a little late. Sara shared with me afterward that when she walked into the room, Steve got up and came over to greet her. The gesture on Steve's part had helped her feel more comfortable.

Of all the projects I worked on with Steve, the most challenging was an endorsement of the Employment Non-Discrimination Act (ENDA). HRC was searching for fair-minded companies willing to endorse the legislation. Prior to the creation of the HRC Business Council they had found a few, but it was the Business Council that successfully took on the task of growing the list. There were a number of factors that made the legislation potentially attractive for corporate endorsement:

- The bill had strong bipartisan support in both houses.
- There were no onerous requirements placed upon corporate America.
- ENDA didn't allow the Equal Employment Opportunity Commission to collect statistics on sexual orientation or compel employers to collect such statistics.
- The bill didn't require employers to provide benefits for same-sex partners of employees.
- ENDA didn't cover businesses with less than 15 employees.

- ENDA would simply and fairly extend the fundamental right to be judged on one's own merits.
- Endorsement of the legislation offered a tangible metric for employers promoting more progressive and inclusive workplace policies.

Still, getting an endorsement wasn't exactly a walk in the daisies. Companies tend to shy away from involvement in legislation not directly pertaining to their business objectives. Some tackle these issues as part of a broader commitment to being a socially responsible business.

Through regular communications I had kept the leadership of my organization well versed on ENDA, its progress, and the potential opportunities for Shell. SEA Shell had done the same with their membership, the Executive Advisory Board, and through educational opportunities. In spite of these efforts, the first attempts were unsuccessful.

I made the first push for an ENDA endorsement in late 1999, starting with the global diversity director and the U.S. diversity leader. They didn't make it easy, with one being located in London and the other in Houston. Finally, an opportunity presented itself in December when all three of us would be in London. The global diversity director suggested a lunch with the U.S. diversity leader to talk about ENDA. They both accepted, only to have last-minute schedule demands derail the opportunity. There were a few reasons why the effort failed:

- Most members of the leadership, including Steve, were just settling into their new roles, making it difficult for them to work on an ENDA endorsement at a time when they were trying to get their arms around their businesses.
- Even though all had risen through the ranks of Shell, most on the leadership team had little or no education or awareness on GLBT workplace issues.

- Shell, like other companies, tended to shy away from politically charged issues not directly pertaining to the business.
- There was no visible broad foundation of support among employees for the endorsement.

Over the next two years the climate changed. The U.S. diversity leader became a real champion for diversity, reviewing metrics and introducing action items regularly during Shell leadership team meetings. Members of the new leadership team settled into their roles on the Executive Advisory Boards for the employee networks.

By the summer of 2001 various members of the Shell leadership team were beginning to feel more at ease with GLBT workplace issues. That summer, for example, SEA Shell had placed posters in the lobby of Shell downtown offices making employees aware of an upcoming Gay Pride event. The building owner had them removed, a distinction not given other employee networks when they placed posters for their events in the lobby. Within a couple of hours, two of Shell's executives were meeting with the building owners—the next morning the posters were again displayed.

In December 2001 Steve keynoted a forum of 50 diversity professionals from 20 corporations on GLBT workplace issues, which Shell hosted. After his remarks Steve stayed for most of the morning session—leaving a very clear message of his commitment to diversity. During the weeks leading up to the forum Steve had been very ill—this was his first engagement back on the job.

The part Steve stayed for was a 90-minute module on gender identity, his first formal training on the topic. He had met Sara, an active member of the SEA Shell steering committee, who was transitioning in the workplace. The module was tag-teamed—I started off with an overview on gender identity, followed by Sara telling her story of what it was like transitioning in the workplace, and then her manager shared what it was like for the business supporting Sara's transition.

I was nervous getting up in front of this audience to present an overview of transgender workplace issues. Not being a subject matter expert, presenting to an audience of external diversity professionals and having one's CEO sitting in the audience can be a little intimidating. There were two thoughts that allowed me to present that day. The first was offered by my team leader during one of our prior discussions—the work we do is a journey, and we can only speak to where we are in our own learning. The second was a prior observation shared by Steve—a leader does some of his best learning when outside his comfort zone.

I was certainly on a journey and out of my comfort zone. Remembering these sage lessons provided the context for my remarks. I simply shared with the audience that little learning time in corporate America is dedicated to transgender workplace issues, I was still in a learning mode, and I would share what I knew based on my journey so far. I had only one desire that day—to be viewed as honest, genuine, and credible in setting the stage for Sara and her supervisor.

I achieved my desired outcome—Sara followed me, talking of her life and struggles to align physically with who she was mentally and emotionally. She spoke to the good times and the not-so-good times. Her supervisor followed, explaining some of the challenges for management and their efforts to do right by Sara.

In the end the message was clear—Sara was a valued employee who should be treated with dignity and respect and allowed to conduct her responsibilities for the company in a safe and productive manner. This very powerful module left a lasting impression with many in the room, including Steve, who would put the knowledge to use in the months to come.

Going back to Sara's transition, with the new millennium came a new face—Ronnie no longer worked for the Deer Park Chemical plant, having been replaced by Sara. To their credit, HR and management did a great job of understanding the transition needs for Ronnie to become Sara full time. After doing their homework, the plant management pulled together the supervisors and explained to them the transition process. I was invited to the meeting—what resonated most for me was the plant manager's insistence that this would be a safe transition for Sara. The transition went smoothly, with the lessons of the chemical plant captured in the gender identity education module shared during the diversity forum Shell had hosted on GLBT workplace issues.

Around the same time of the diversity forum, I was made aware of another push for ENDA endorsements. The U.S. Senate subcommittee on Health, Education, Labor and Pensions (HELP) was administering hearings on ENDA in February 2002. Invitations were sent to several companies, including Shell, inviting testimony from the CEO. While having a good working relationship with Steve, I wanted to be considerate to his direct reports, offering them the opportunity to share the news with him.

In my correspondence with these leaders I provided background on ENDA, how supporting the legislation aligned with the business strategy and values of the company, and an electronic copy of the most current version of the bill. I had also done my homework—people with the HRC WorkNet Project explained various scenarios for offering testimony in the event the CEO could not attend in person. I also found a wealth of experience available on format, content, and distribution of testimony for such a Senate hearing.

Over the course of several weeks I briefed the U.S. diversity leader. His inquiries were helpful in developing the appropriate package of materials for briefing other leaders and identifying those leaders who would have a vested interest. The U.S. diversity leader shared that Steve could not give testimony at the hearing because he would be in London that day. From my conversations with HRC, I knew he didn't have to be there—his testimony could be submitted in writing and read into the record. Given this insight, I continued my briefings for leaders on the HELP subcommittee hearing.

As January 2002 came and went, I was becoming concerned —the leaders were receiving regular updates on the Senate subcommittee hearing, but I was getting no feedback. When I spoke with my team leader about the situation, he understood my frustration and suggested a modification to my approach. He suggested talking with a leader not directly involved to understand what the obstacles might be to making progress on ENDA.

The logical choice that popped into my mind was the general counsel. Cathy was someone I respected and admired. For someone of her rank and status, she was approachable and open to listening, and she shared practical insights. During our meeting I explained the situation concerning ENDA and provided her with the briefing documents. She showed a genuine interest, asking that I forward copies of ENDA to an attorney in the legal practice and the HR manager responsible for Equal Employment Opportunity (EEO). She also suggested trying to call the vice president of government affairs again the next morning.

The next morning copies of ENDA were off to the appropriate people, and before I could pick up the phone to call Government Affairs, they called my office. Literally overnight, an ENDA endorsement began moving through the proper channels for approval. EEO and Legal found the legislation agreeable. I took a shot at formulating a draft of the testimony content. Steve reviewed and offered changes to the text, which was forwarded to Government Affairs, appropriately formatted, and distributed to the U.S. Senate HELP Subcommittee prior to the meeting. The message sent by the supporting testimony was very clear:

> Society today is demanding greater accountability from businesses, governments, and individuals. Shell's commitment is to America—and what it represents. And the Employment Non-Discrimination Act goes to the core of what

this nation is all about. Giving all our citizens the fundamental right to be judged on one's own merits.

After years of failed attempts, Shell had finally endorsed ENDA, and I was beat. After the heart attack I had lost some of my stamina. It was harder to put in the long hours and late nights. This wasn't the only thing I was working on, cutting into my personal time and commitments, but it was the most important thing for me personally. It was very physically, emotionally and mentally draining to pursue interests in which others do not readily see value. Persistence requires an enormous amount of patience and energy.

At the time Shell was the only major energy company endorsing the legislation. Within weeks Lord John Brown was giving a speech promoting diversity and inclusion at a meeting in Berlin, Germany. To the surprise of many, an endorsement of ENDA had been worked into the speech. How the endorsement from BP came about has remained a mystery to me. It's obvious to me BP saw the value proposition and wanted to punctuate their position with the GLBT community.

Several years prior, when first introduced to ENDA, I could rationalize the benefits and business case for companies to support the legislation. I pursued the effort of an ENDA endorsement because I recognized the opportunity for a company to tangibly demonstrate leadership in creating a safe, open workplace where everyone had the right to achieve his or her full potential.

ENDA wasn't the only activity tied to the GLBT community that was in play at the time. The co-chairs for the Houston HRC dinner held in March 2002 were from the Shell and Alliance GLBT employee networks (SEA Shell & Prism). They had invited Steve to be the honorary chair of the event, and he accepted. By this time Steve had all the credentials because of his support of various GLBT-friendly local and state policies and legislation in

Texas. The ENDA endorsement gave him a standing on the national stage as well.

My role in Steve's HRC dinner appearance was making it happen. The co-chairs relied upon me to coordinate efforts between the Media Relations and External Affairs staff. What goes into such a production is astounding—putting the event on the calendars of Steve's leadership team, letters inviting other corporate leaders, invitations for local and state government officials, the speech preparations, news briefs and talking points.

It's still rare to find a CEO in Houston with Steve's record of promoting inclusion. I felt his record warranted more visibility then just an honorary chair at a dinner. So I approached Greg Jeu, the publisher of *Out Smart* magazine, about doing an interview with Steve that would come out in their March issue. Hearing a list of Steve's accomplishments, Greg was excited about the idea and asked the executive director of the Greater Houston GLBT Chamber of Commerce to do the interview and write the story.

The interview was scheduled to be a conference call in early February—Steve asked if my team leader and I would be present in the event he needed a little "depth on the bench." I took the invitation as quite an honor—after all, it's not every day the CEO invites you to a meeting.

The interview went without a hitch. Steve did a great job. There was no need for me to jump in to support the effort, yet he invited me to do so by redirecting one of the questions for my comment. In response I shared my thoughts at that moment—six years prior, when I had come out at work, I never thought of one day sitting in a conference room with the CEO of Shell having an interview with *Out Smart* magazine. All those years ago Richard had been right—publishing my coming out story had changed my life in ways I couldn't imagine. Sitting there with Steve was proof.

Although I had worked diligently on the ENDA Endorsement, Shell's support of GLBT friendly policies at the city and state level, Elizabeth's keynote of the Shell Diversity conference, and preparing the CEO for the Houston HRC dinner, there was no room for Slava or me at the dinner. Literally up until the day before the event, we weren't going to attend, when miraculously two seats appeared at a far-off table. Slava and I arrived smartly dressed in tuxedoes and wearing our matching opal earrings.

I had redrafted the remarks read by the co-chair to introduce Steve. They simply outlined his achievements to date in support of the GLBT community—the response to his ascending the stage was a standing ovation from over 1,000 people. I was very proud of Steve, and I was also pleased that the audience gave him his due when he reached the podium. During the speech he received additional applause, and another standing ovation at the close. He had proved once again that people, not corporate whim, are responsible for creating meaningful change.

Life at work settled down after the Houston HRC dinner. I was acting on my interest in moving on with my career, and during the month of May I noticed a posting that I chose to pursue. The assignment offered a promotion, a management title, and the opportunity to blend my environmental and diversity skills.

Before leaving there was one last opportunity to work with Steve. He had been invited to speak at Dell Computer as part of a June kickoff for their GLBT employee network. He would be going up with Pat, the VP of Tax, who was a member of the SEA Shell Executive Advisory Board. I was on point to prepare Steve's remarks and coordinate with Pat. Steve was going to speak from the perspective of a business leader. Pat would speak to his experience as a SEA Shell advisor and parent of a gay child. The combination was a very powerful message.

I had offered up my team leader and myself as being available should Steve and Pat feel they needed a little depth on the bench, and they accepted the offer. Having other things he wanted to do that day, my team leader wasn't crazy about spending half the day in Austin, but I just wanted him to get a little more grounding on the topic in front of a big audience.

This was another opportunity for my team leader to be exposed to the different facets of sexual orientation as a focus area of diversity. Having him attend the *Out Smart* interview with Steve was another. He struggled with my including him in these activities, as they were disruptive to his schedule. But I wanted to further his learning journey on GLBT workplace issues. I was pretty certain that after I left the Diversity Practice, no one was going to continue pressing the team to learn more in this area.

The day of the event we all met at the Shell hangar. I had never been on a corporate jet before. Throughout my career I had made a point of avoiding them, having a sense the atmosphere created by the passengers would be very uncomfortable. Steve and Pat quickly dispelled my apprehensions. As the highest-ranking official on the plane, Steve was the flight attendant—I'm not used to being served breakfast by the CEO.

Upon arrival in Austin we were whisked off to Dell, greeted by their diversity director, and spent a little time with Michael Dell before the program. Michael had a very appealing personality, gracious and connected with those in the room, yet unable to release himself from the pressing business issues awaiting on the other side of the conference room door. I admired his giving time to this event, even though I was quite certain he wouldn't stay.

At the appointed time we were escorted to the main meeting room, where a few hundred people had congregated for the presentation. I had chosen a black Armani sport coat and slacks for the occasion, and true to form, was wearing my opal earring. We were seated in the front row while Michael took the stage to introduce Steve. From where we were seated I could see some of the leaders of the Dell GLBT network. They seemed eager to hear what Steve and Pat had to share.

Steve started off talking about respect, honesty, fairness and decency as the values that still power the world. He shared insights on the role he saw for business: being influential and modeling inclusivity. Steve attributed the success of Shell's diversity efforts up to that point to a series of contributing factors:

- Leadership demonstrated a visible commitment to diversity goals and the agenda.
- For several years Shell had been offering extensive diversity awareness and education programs in all the businesses.
- Shell had set specific goals and devised formal measures to track progress in achieving a balanced workforce.
- Succession planning was linked to the diversity agenda.
- Shell established diversity leadership in the businesses and a Diversity Practice reporting to the CEO that served as both a resource and a catalyst for change.
- Managers at all levels were responsible for diversity and evaluated on their progress toward diversity goals in their performance assessments.

One role of employee networks was to help the company model policies and practices to the external world. They became an invaluable resource as conduits for communication among employees and management. By this time SEA Shell was participating in the Houston AIDS walk, the Gay Pride parade, and events for the Greater Houston GLBT Chamber. SEA Shell had been guiding the Shell Oil Company Foundation in targeting donations to organizations serving the GLBT community and served as advisors to leadership on the Boy Scouts/United Way issue, James Byrd Jr. Hate Crimes legislation, and the city of Houston's efforts to add sexual orientation to their non-discrimination policy.

Steve went on talking about Elizabeth Birch's speech at the Shell Diversity conference, being the honorary chair of the Houston HRC dinner, interviewing with *Out Smart* magazine, endorsing ENDA, and Shell's making the *Advocate* magazine list of best companies for gays and lesbians. I periodically glanced over at the leaders for the Dell GLBT group, noticing that they seemed very pleased with Steve's accomplishments.

Pat followed, talking about his role as an advisor to SEA Shell and the journey and learning for him personally. Up to that point he would look in the mirror while shaving in the morning and ask himself, "Am I treating people the way I would want to be treated?" Through involvement in SEA Shell and lessons from his daughter, Pat found himself changing the question to, "Am I treating people the way they would want to be treated?" This is a much tougher question to answer, implying that one has to know the people in order to know how they wish to be treated.

Pat also did something that surprised me—he launched head on into putting the issue of beliefs vs. behaviors squarely on the table by making a point about tolerance vs. inclusion. He talked to his own beliefs, his love for his daughter, and treating her the way she wished to be treated. In the workplace he emphasized everyone being treated with dignity and respect, creating an environment where all employees felt they had a real chance to exercise their creativity, knowledge and experience without fear of ostracism or reprisal. The message was clear—this wasn't about creating a tolerant environment, but an inclusive one.

I was very proud to be an employee of Shell that day. During the Q&A session that followed, Steve and Pat teamed up on stage. Questions touched on the value proposition for networks, how they were formed, and their usefulness. I thought I'd have a pretty relaxing time of it, watching them do all the work, but then came that one question about how networks translated globally.

Steve glanced in my direction and I was on my feet, headed for the stage. In Shell there were no "global networks"—there were other networks elsewhere in the world. The sensitivity was around the reality that some of the networks would be illegal in some countries (e.g. women's network, GLBT network). Shell as a global business had to operate within the laws in those parts of the world. Following on my lead, Steve had a chance to add a few thoughts regarding his personal experiences in some of those other parts of the world.

I stayed with them for the rest of the question session. There was only one more question with which I assisted—what was the relationship between Shell and the HRC and how effective was this relationship? Steve and Pat deferred the question to me. I expressed that Shell had a strong working relationship with the HRC, as illustrated by Steve's role as honorary chair of the Houston HRC dinner and Elizabeth Birch's keynoting the Shell Diversity Conference. I further added that my role on the HRC Business Council helped cement the relationship.

Afterward, many in attendance thanked us for making time to meet with them. Even some former Shell employees who were working for Dell stopped by to say hello. They seemed to admire most the progress achieved by an oil and gas company, I think hoping Dell would one day follow suit.

The plane ride back was very eventful. Everyone was checking BlackBerrys, reconnecting with the workplace that was set aside for the few hours we were at Dell. Among the e-mails, Steve had been copied on some traffic between the Chairman of the Royal Dutch/Shell Group and the head of Human Resources. The notes were in response to a message from an employee at a refinery in Canada. The employee was outing himself as transgender and relaying plans to transition from male to female over the coming months.

The correspondence between the chairman and HR suggested a level of uncertainty in how to address the issue, with the HR executive advising caution based on decade-old experiences with a previous employer. Steve was in a fortunate position—at 30,000 feet, he had a thought leader on GLBT workplace issues sitting with him on the plane. Just six months prior, Steve had participated in a module on issues pertaining to gender identity in the workplace.

After some discussion on the plane, drawing on his knowledge from previous education, Steve entered the dialogue. Sending a note to everyone on the distribution, Steve offered up that Shell had experience with transgender workplace issues in the U.S. and would connect the appropriate people in Houston with their counterparts in Canada.

It was a classic example of Steve implementing a lesson he had shared with me when we first met—one does his best learning when he steps out of his comfort zone. Steve had stepped out of his comfort zone to understand GLBT workplace issues and there, right before my eyes, had applied the learning with the ease and self-assurance that comes with being an effective leader.

I believe change has to be visible, and not necessarily the change agent. Some of my most enduring legacies were imprinted on the systems and processes of the company, yet brought little focus or attention to me or to others who were crafting the changes. For example, the online training for harassment in the workplace referenced the nondiscrimination policy for the company. The software was "off the shelf" and addressed those groups currently covered against discrimination by federal law (e.g. race, religion, sex, disability, veterans, etc.).

While taking the online training, I noticed it wasn't aligned with the nondiscrimination policy statement of the company—specifically, the training mentioned nothing about sexual orientation. Realizing this was probably an oversight not caught by those implementing the software, I sent a note to the VP of Legal, the compliance officer for Shell, my team leader, and the U.S. diversity leader raising the observation.

In some companies such a note might be overlooked or dismissed. In this instance I found people coming to my office seeking recommendations for correcting the error. Within a few weeks the software modifications were up and running. For me this was a tangible sign of the continuing progress of the company to be inclusive.

My tour of duty in the Shell Diversity Practice ended on the 14th of August, 2002, just shy of four years. My new assignment brought with it a promotion and the opportunity to blend my experience in environment and diversity. Reflecting back on my time in the Diversity Center/Practice, there were some significant signs of progress and lessons learned:

- People really do create change when faced with a challenge. Because of other priorities, GLBT employee issues hadn't been a strong plank in Shell's diversity platform prior to my entering the Practice. This slowly changed through measured persistence and patience.
    - More diversity education offerings were adding sexual orientation.
    - Some senior leaders were coming on board with GLBT workplace issues and were more comfortable responding to both the issues and opportunities.
    - While not requested to, I had provided regular updates on issues that could impact the workplace (e.g. ENDA, ExxonMobil's dropping GLBT-friendly policies, and the BSA).
    - I had supportive mentors and leaders interested in expanding their personal learning and SEA Shell's work on education.
- Employee networks were becoming invaluable conduits for promoting communication among employees and management, and served as advisors to leadership on issues affecting the workplace.
- Through quarterly exchanges the CEO was able to effectively connect with the grassroots portion of the organization, in essence helping to build broader consensus supporting decision-making and learning.

- Putting someone in an awkward situation or creating a sense of discomfort is not conducive to learning. Sara's being comfortable in a meeting with the CEO was important to the learning experiences of all involved.
- If at first you don't succeed, try, try again. Persistence requires an enormous amount of patience and energy. Sometimes first attempts aren't successful.
- Obtaining an ENDA endorsement required working within established channels, not circumventing them. Getting plugged into the channels can at times be a challenge. Having credibility with senior leaders is helpful in navigating these channels.
- Stowing my personal "baggage" and demonstrating my willingness to create a clean slate gave the new Diversity Center leader the opportunity to demonstrate his commitment without having to continually justify his past.
- When called upon to brief leaders on workplace issues, I tried to be as objective as possible, sharing my thoughts and the potential benefits and weighing the possible risks. When discussing risks, I provided suggestions for their mitigation. I tried to summarize the reality of the situation, offering options rather than a single recommendation.
- In his role Steve provided visionary leadership and a framework within which the businesses could operate effectively by:
    - Concisely laying out the values and general business directives of the company.
    - Establishing key planks for achieving success, among them a commitment to diversity & inclusion.

    - Talking about respect, honesty, fairness and decency as the values that still power the world.

- Supporting Steve's responses to inquiries about diversity and inclusion opened my eyes to a couple of key observations:
    - It's important to have a meaningful business case for inclusion of sexual orientation and gender identity in the diversity efforts of a company.
    - This wasn't about personal values—it was about expected behaviors and treating people with dignity and respect.

- When presenting materials on topics on which I did not always consider myself an expert, I kept three things in the back of my mind:
    - The work we do is a journey, and we can only speak to where we are in our own learning.
    - A leader does some of his or her best learning when outside his or her comfort zone.
    - My only desire was to be viewed as honest, genuine, and credible.

- My team leader made the observation that we're all on a learning journey and we can only speak to where we are on that path. Inviting him to join me for the *Out Smart* interview and the Dell meeting was an effort on my part to move him a little further down the path and to encourage him to speak a little more.

- Building an effective working relationship with a CEO and his leadership team takes time and patience—credibility isn't given freely, it's something you earn.

- Learning is a two-way street, affected by the willingness of parties involved to agree to grow together. Steve and I both grew in our knowledge and understanding of the workplace because we were both engaged in learning from our experiences.

11 The Reality of Change

Determining what should be the next assignment on my career path hadn't been easy. Unlike some in the businesses, I had no "skill pool manager" watching over my career. Skill pool managers advised engineers and geologists on potential next steps in their careers. In fact, I was "pond jumping," moving from one skill pool to another. I had a vision of growing through the ranks to achieve a senior executive role in a company. Although I had many of the leadership skills and competencies, there wasn't a clear path identified for my progression. For the first time in my life I was making decisions about my future without really being able to see where they might take me ten years down the road.

Conversations with my team leader and the U.S. diversity leader provided little in the way of guidance or direction. It was pretty clear that I had to figure it out for myself. I created a list of fundamental desires—the new position would have to build on my environmental, diversity, and leadership competencies and skills. Up to this point I had had no formal management title, something I wanted to change. My next supervisor had to be comfortable with my sexual orientation, and if possible, I wanted to go back into a business.

I had been reviewing internal job postings for a few months when an ideal opportunity presented itself—Sustainable Development (SD) Manager, Corporate Affairs. The job met most of my requirements, but wasn't in a business. Corporate Affairs had new leadership and had just completely restructured. The SD position was part of a new department, and I would have staff and budget.

Applying for the position was tougher then the interview process—it felt like climbing a mountain. The hiring manager had requested my last three performance evaluations. Neither HR nor my team leader could produce all three. I had kept final drafts, but not signed-off versions. In fact, my HR file was empty—all they had was an electronic version of my last evaluation. My supervisor and I spent a couple of days recreating the other two evaluations from my final drafts and notes.

My work in diversity had helped me gain name recognition among the senior leaders of Shell. Some had written recommendations on my behalf, and even the CEO told me afterward that he had put in a good word. This didn't hurt me during the culling process, as I became one of the three finalists interviewed for the position.

I was vacationing in Idaho at the time and maneuvered most of the interviews via phone. Upon my return I had a face-to-face meeting with the hiring manager. During our meeting we talked about a number of things, including my sexual orientation. I brought the topic up in conversation to assure it wouldn't be a surprise after the fact should I get the position. She seemed okay with the revelation of having a gay manager in her department.

About a day after the meeting, a manager called, informing me the hiring manager was checking references. During the discussion the hiring manager had asked my reference how my sexual orientation had affected my job performance. The reference responded by saying I was very professional and business-focused when conducting meetings with clients. The reference suggested that the hiring manager raise the question with me, as I would be very comfortable having the discussion.

There was no further conversation. My supervisor chose to leave my sexual orientation an "undiscussable"—ever present in the room, but not a topic of conversation. By not bringing up the topic, the hiring manager was able to exert some sense of control of the situation that would prevent possible embarrassment for both of us.

A few days later I received a call formally offering me the position. I didn't bring up the conversation the hiring manager had had with one of my references. Instead, I let it lie—there would be many opportunities for my new supervisor to view my performance in front of the businesses.

Corporate Affairs had always been a "strange animal" even when I was their diversity consultant. The organization was positioned as the internal/external conscience for the company's operations in the U.S. The restructuring was undertaken with the objective of realigning Corporate Affairs to better support the businesses. As a result, a number of people from the businesses had moved into positions in the new organization.

There were other changes ongoing. Steve retired a couple of weeks after I assumed my new responsibilities. After retiring he offered to have lunch with me now and then, an opportunity I didn't want to waste. How many people get a chance to learn from a well-respected CEO?

One cannot predict the future—just make the best of each day and acknowledge the challenges imposed by the environment. After assuming my new responsibilities, I quickly learned more about the culture of Corporate Affairs. While a diversity consultant, I was encouraged to meet with business leaders. In my new assignment there were those who were very protective of access to leadership. The best description would be a "kiss up—kick down" management style. I worked well with most in the various functions, but the work environment was unlike anything I had ever been exposed to in my career. People were very competitive, and why not? Shortly after taking the new assignment, Corporate Affairs leadership announced another staffing exercise.

During the two-year assignment there were two more restructuring efforts, and I went through two supervisors. The staff I was to have hired never materialized, the budget was significantly reduced, and the spending authority was tightly controlled by superiors. In spite of the challenges, I tried to make the most of the situation. I also expended significant amounts of energy steering clear of the traps and politics, wanting to rise above it all and concentrate on the job at hand. I found myself struggling to keep commitments as a member of the HRC Business Council and had dropped out of most leadership positions in other community organizations. Giving up the Business Council role was not something I relished—the group was inspiring and supportive. Yet I felt my supervisor would be happier if I stepped down.

Most of the time I felt vulnerable and challenged when doing anything beyond my work as the SD manager. At times it felt like the SD manager role was 24/7. My general perception was that if something wasn't part of the job, I shouldn't be involved in it. For instance, the Shell Diversity Practice had submitted my candidacy for the Trailblazer Award given at the Out & Equal Workplace Issues Conference. Everyone has heard of the Oscars, Emmys, and Tonys—well, these are the "Outties."

The Shell Diversity Practice called to share that I had been selected as one of five finalists and invited to be at the conference for the award presentation. I was very surprised—this was very unexpected. No one had ever made the effort to nationally recognize my contributions to creating a safe, open workplace for GLBT employees. I asked about others on the list, and as the names were rattled off, I also realized I wasn't going to win.

During my life there have been a rare few people I've looked up to as role models and admired. One of them was on the list: Louise from Raytheon. Louise and I had met through the HRC Business Council, which she and I co-chaired for a year. During our years on the business council we became good friends, and I had learned so much from her insights and experience. I knew she would win.

I really wanted to go, yet I knew Corporate Affairs wouldn't support sending me unless I won. So I chose not to press the issue. The event came and passed—as I had surmised, Louise received the award. My only regret was not having been there with her to share in the happiness she so richly deserved. I was personally disappointed by the ambivalence of Corporate Affairs, an organization that didn't value my contributions to creating a safe and inclusive workplace.

There was a silver lining to the day—SEA Shell won an "Outtie" that year for its work as an employee network group. I was very proud of the people who had had a hand in making SEA Shell successful. The seeds I had helped sow years prior had matured and borne fruit.

I took advantage of Steve's offer to periodically have lunch together after he retired. Those lunches were highlights for me—he had so much to share and the real experiences to support the lessons. Steve and I had one last trip together after he retired. He was receiving a CEO leadership award in Washington, D.C. Steve's speech was a plea for businesses to pay more attention to underrepresented minorities. While not a topic of his speech, Steve erred in referring to "sexual preference" as part of a broader definition of diversity instead of sexual orientation. People who think sexual orientation is a choice—not exactly where I perceived Steve to be on the topic—often use the term sexual preference.

I couldn't let go of the words "sexual preference"—finding myself dwelling on the remark and becoming somewhat irritated. I think what triggered my irritation was the work environment in which I found myself. After years of progress in creating a more open and inclusive workplace, I was right back at the beginning. My new assignment was in an organization that managed to stave off working the topic of sexual orientation as an element of inclusion.

Finally, I took a deep breath, realizing this wasn't about Steve. It was just a mistake, and I'd coach him on it later. What troubled me most was the anger welling within—I could only attribute the feeling to a subconscious reflex triggered by the current work environment in which I found myself. The long days, high stress, and organizational restructuring seemed to be taking a toll on my patience. Steve's slipping up normally wouldn't be something to make me irritated.

On the return flight I had a chance to talk with Steve. I highlighted what I had really liked about his speech, then asked permission to give him a little coaching. He agreed, and I politely emphasized losing the phrase "sexual preference," reminding him it wasn't my preference to be gay. I did this in a forward manner, injecting some humor into the situation—we both laughed and he agreed to revisit his lexicon.

As Steve offered his experience in support of my learning, I made a personal decision to support him whenever the need arose. For example, a month after the Washington, D.C., trip I received a frantic call from Steve's secretary. He was up for an award from the Greater Houston GLBT Chamber of Commerce. The event was only ten days off and not on Steve's schedule—there was a "hold the date" request, but no one had followed up confirming the speaking engagement. Steve and his secretary heard about the event from an e-mail congratulating him on the award.

Having close ties with the Chamber, I made some calls. They had been advertising a luncheon downtown where they would present the GLBT Chamber's first Straight Ally award, and Steve was the recipient. I called Steve's secretary back, explaining the situation and exploring options. Steve was traveling up until the day of the event and was unlikely to be prepared to give a speech.

The Chamber is an organization I've always supported and believed in from the beginning. This was their first annual award luncheon, and I wanted to support Steve and salvage the event. Sticking my neck way out, I offered to prepare a draft speech if Steve would look at it. I got lucky—a few days before the event Steve's secretary told me he liked the speech. He was going to make some changes to the text and do the event. The director for the Chamber breathed a huge sigh of relief and asked that I introduce Steve during the event.

There were about 150 people attending the luncheon. Introducing Steve, I highlighted his major efforts as a leader and shared a couple of things I had learned while working with him: 1) As a leader it's important to have a broad foundation of support when making decisions, and 2) As a leader you do some of your best learning when you step out of your comfort zone. Both lessons I continue to apply again and again.

True to form, the people in the room welcomed Steve with a standing ovation. He seemed so comfortable on stage—moving through his record supporting the GLBT community and sharing what he had learned along the journey. He even found a place in his remarks to thank me for helping in his development and growth as a leader. I was very proud of Steve—he had learned how to "dance" and wasn't stepping on a single toe.

The relationship I have with Steve is very unique—no CEO I worked under at Shell, before or after, had mastered diversity and inclusion in quite the same way. With Steve's successors came changes to the focus of the CEO role in the U.S. They wore two hats: CEO of Shell Oil Company, and president of a major Shell business in the U.S.

The time I spent in Corporate Affairs had a noticeable impact on my physical well-being. A few months after accepting the role in Corporate Affairs, I made a visit to my doctor, who made the observation that the stress level I was dealing with was readily apparent. If I didn't take action to manage the stress, he was going to. I convinced him that conditions at work were going to improve.

Shortly thereafter I got a new boss. Instead of reporting to a director, I reported to a vice president—the result of the latest restructuring of Corporate Affairs. Not much else changed. She professed support for creating a diverse and inclusive workplace and integrated a learning piece into each of our quarterly department meetings. On occasion she'd solicit my advice on possible topics—sexual orientation was never on the list, as she felt the group was "nowhere near ready" for the subject. This intrigued me because I was not in the closet in my assignment, my boyfriend's picture was on my desk, and many in Corporate Affairs knew I was gay and seemed to be coping.

Another comment she conveyed was that I could feel "safe" on her leadership team. I didn't want to be "safe" on a leadership team. I wanted to work in a safe, open work environment where I was treated with dignity and respect and had the opportunity to achieve my potential. There was nothing occurring in Corporate Affairs that even came close to creating this type of work environment. This was very surprising to me, because the U.S. Diversity Office had been moved into Corporate Affairs after Steve's retirement. The U.S. diversity leader had moved on to explore opportunities elsewhere. A director reporting to the executive vice president of Corporate Affairs who in turn reported to the CEO had replaced him. This was the first time Diversity did not have a direct reporting function to the CEO.

I didn't feel supported in my development needs while in Corporate Affairs. There appeared to be no interest in developing my management skills—I had requested to enroll in a management training program, only to have the request declined by my supervisor. I couldn't help but feel unsupported and often wondered if my supervisor's behavior had anything to do with my sexual orientation.

One thing was apparent—Corporate Affairs would be my last assignment with Shell. The organization seemed to be continually recreating itself. Under these conditions I got the impression that investing in people was apparently a risky proposition, given the investment might be gone within a few months.

By the end of 2003 I made some conscious decisions about the coming year. I was going to rejoin the steering team for SEA Shell. I wanted first-hand knowledge of their challenges, to become connected with the leaders and reconnected with a part of my identity denied in Corporate Affairs. I felt any meaningful legacy I had left to create at Shell would come through SEA Shell. So that was where I wanted to focus my creative efforts and energy in hopes of leaving a lasting impression in the company.

I had completed every task on my personal agenda relative to my GLBT legacy with one exception—having gender identity added to the nondiscrimination policy. With each restructuring of Corporate Affairs came a round of packages—I knew a round was coming in March 2004, but my plan was to take one later in the year. I was pretty certain another round would follow.

The toughest question I had to answer for myself was whether I could walk away from Shell, the benefits, and the paycheck. It took a great deal of courage for me to admit to myself that the direction of the organization was not aligned with my values.

I reflected on a conversation I had had with a friend on the HRC Business Council. She had shared with me over a beer that her employer had decided to shift direction on the business strategy—she had the option of shifting with them or stepping down, allowing someone else to lead in her place. After asking herself whether she had the energy, drive and interest to pursue the new direction, she honestly had to answer "no." I admired most her courage and her ability to honest with herself.

With my decision made, I began to take on the objectives I felt important to complete in the timetable available. Getting gender identity into the Shell non-discrimination policy became a priority. SEA Shell had a Gender Identity sub-committee assigned to the task—they just needed a little momentum. I joined the team and we began to pursue the task of creating a briefing document for the Shell leadership team.

I drafted an outline for the briefing document; then everyone pitched in, taking a piece to work on, and over a few weeks the document began to take shape. Throughout the process briefings were given to the SEA Shell Steering Team and EAB. A member of the new Diversity Center in Corporate Affairs was affiliated with the EAB and the SEA Shell steering team, but rarely attended the meetings.

By mid-summer the document was done, and members of the subcommittee and the SEA Shell EAB took the document to the CEO. There were three possible outcomes: 1) The CEO agreed with the recommendations, notified her leadership team, and made the change; 2) The CEO made the recommendations a topic on an agenda for the leadership team to discuss; or 3) The CEO disagreed with the recommendations and dropped the issue.

As it played out, the CEO went with the second option. This gave the Gender Identity sub-committee an opportunity to approach their business leadership prior to the meeting. Through past relationships, I took the opportunity to meet with the leaders from Corporate Affairs and Legal. I was very surprised by the conversations—both seemed reluctant to support the change.

I had a sense that something had happened with the leadership team under the direction of the new CEO. I was not aware of the CEO's having supported GLBT workplace issues in the past, so there was no tangible record. She was very business driven—I wasn't seeing evidence to suggest diversity and inclusion were high on her agenda. I think this change of direction may have had the effect of eroding the commitment to diversity and inclusion from others on the team.

I discovered later on the day of the Shell leadership team meeting that many of the team members had sent alternates in their places. Apparently, if the business leader couldn't make the meeting, they sent someone else. As it turned out, even the CEO had sent an alternate. Rather than the decision-makers for the business deciding the fate of including gender identity in the company non-discrimination policy, it was left to the alternates. Their decision was to not add gender identity, offering instead to direct HR to review their policies to assure they could address gender identity issues in the workplace when they occurred.

Sara was among the most disappointed. The policy change would have given her and others something tangible to grasp when challenging discriminatory behavior, and the company would have policies in place to address gender transitioning in the workplace.

Afterward, during a conversation with the leader of Corporate Affairs, I said that the decision of the leadership team meant that Shell would not reach a score of 100 on the HRC Corporate Equality Index. In response I was told the HRC Corporate Equality Index was not a metric the leadership was interested in achieving. The climate for GLBT workplace equality felt like it was slowly eroding away.

As a postscript to these events, in 2005, ChevronTexaco and BP became the first energy companies to add gender identity to their non-discrimination policies. Both companies have scores of 100 on the HRC Corporate Equality Index. It would be almost another four years before Shell finally changed the policy. Just recently (April 2008) I heard from Sara that the company nondiscrimination policy had finally been revised to include gender identity.

By fall of 2004, shortly after losing the pitch to add gender identity to the Shell non-discrimination policy, the results of another restructuring of Corporate Affairs were announced and another round of packages was forthcoming. Shortly after the announcement, my supervisor pulled me aside after a meeting at Rice

University to break the news that my position was being eliminated. I had 90 days to find another job or take the package. She was rather shocked at how well I took the news. The packages were right on time—why wouldn't I take it well?

Interestingly, when I received the materials I noticed the "Release and Settlement" agreement wording did not conform to the wording in Shell's nondiscrimination policy—they'd left out sexual orientation. Not having explored this part of the HR systems and policies in the past, I hadn't had the opportunity to review and comment on the document. So in good faith I sent a note off to my supervisor, the leader of Corporate Affairs, and the head of Legal, pointing out the deficiency. I never received a written reply to my inquiry from anyone. The only feedback came from my supervisor, whom I believe talked to HR, who had talked to Legal, relaying that they felt they were covered by the wording that existed in the agreement.

I really enjoyed my last three months in the office. For the first time in my career I was coming in at 6:30 a.m. and going home by 4:30 p.m. I took care of the business that was most pressing and began to think through the handoff of my assignments to others. Even Slava could sense I was feeling better about things. I wasn't grouchy and stressed when I came home. There was never an opportunity while in Corporate Affairs for Slava to meet any of my supervisors, nor did I have a sense he really wanted to meet them.

In early October I had made one last trip to Washington, D.C., for an HRC Business Council meeting. Prior to the meeting I met with Daryl, who oversaw the Business Council. Over coffee I shared a desire for this to be my last meeting. I didn't want him to say anything or have anything on the agenda—I just wanted to go to the meeting like in the past, do my part, and leave—I'm not big on good-byes.

My reasons for leaving the Business Council were several. I knew I'd be on a fixed income over the course of the next year or so and wanted to limit expenses where I could. After seven years on the council, I wanted to allow others the opportunity to be on the team. I wouldn't be far away—always willing to support the efforts of the Business Council in any manner HRC saw fit. I never walked away from the people—I made some good friends and shared some wonderful memories.

My last duty for Corporate Affairs was a workshop on sexual orientation and gender identity. Their Diversity Council, with the prodding of one member in particular, was going to offer a "Lunch and Learn" session on the topic, and I was asked to co-facilitate. The date finally selected was in early December. The rationale for the date was finding a time that fit the agendas of the Corporate Affairs leadership team so they could attend.

I worked with my co-facilitator from the Corporate Affairs Diversity Council on the design of the session. Around 50 people signed up for the event and confirmed, including most of the leadership team. When the day finally arrived, about half of those confirmed actually showed up for the session. Of those that made it, only one member of the Corporate Affairs leadership team was present.

In spite of the turnout, we did the workshop. Those in the room found it to be a very valuable learning experience. I wasn't hurt or disappointed by the turnout—it was really what I had expected. By now the behavior of the leadership team was fairly predictable. I would have been surprised had they all been in the room.

Afterward I sent an e-mail to the leadership team, first thanking them for supporting the offering of the workshop. I further noted that their absence was very visible, and while supporting the workshop sends a message, so does their lack of attendance. That got me an all-expense-paid trip to the office of the HR manager. The HR manager appreciated the note and explained that they had been all called away at the last minute for an important meeting. I realize last minute events do come up and shared that knowing why they weren't there didn't change the message for those in the organization. It was at this point that she realized they should have rescheduled the "Lunch and Learn" rather than let it proceed without the participation of the leadership—a lesson.

With my days at Shell coming to a close, I dedicated most of my time to lunches with old friends, cleaning out my office, and passing off my work to others. In November my cardiologist decided to take a look at my heart to see how things were going. What he saw was a scarred stent. This news resulted in shorter workdays for the rest of the year and into early January to take advantage of a procedure to alleviate the problem.

My supervisor had come into my office late in November to share that she'd be gone most of the month and probably wouldn't see me again before I departed. I smiled and assured her it was no big deal—it was actually what I had expected. The conversation reinforced why I was leaving. I do believe there is still an opportunity to observe lessons even in an undesirable work environment:

- Change is not something that comes uniformly to all parts of the company. Only through education and a standing commitment from generations of leadership is change woven into the fabric of a company culture.

- After leaving the Diversity Practice, I moved into a work environment where my sexual orientation became an undiscussable. People knew I was gay, but no one was going to talk about it.

- Steve's use of "sexual preference" demonstrates how working to become inclusive and respectful is a journey and not a "quick fix." His being open to coaching was, in my mind, a sign of a true leader.

- I had the courage to admit to myself that the direction Shell was taking was not aligned with my values and it was time for me to move on.

- The process of building credibility with a new CEO takes patience and time. The rapid rotation of CEOs for Shell in the U.S. between 2002 and 2005 made it impossible for me to build a meaningful and mutually respectful relationship to support their learning about sexual orientation and gender identity.

After Steve retired, there was a loss of momentum on GLBT workplace issues, with shifting commitments and priorities for the new leaders. I was left with a perception that the focus going forward would be more on the business and less on people.

- The leadership team for Corporate Affairs sent a message to the organization by scheduling a sexual orientation learning session. They also sent a message by their absence at the session. What leaders advocate and how they behave are viewed and interpreted by others in the organization.

- I don't want to be part of a leadership team that's "safe." I want to be part of a safe, productive work environment that treats everyone with dignity and respect and encourages people to achieve their potential.

My career with Shell ended on December 31, 2004. On the morning of January 1, 2005, I got up, went to the kitchen, and pulled out a pint of Ben & Jerry's Chocolate Chip Cookie Dough ice cream (compliments of a manager from Ben & Jerry's) and a bottle of Dom Perignon. I took both into the living room, settled down in front of the fireplace, and enjoyed the peace and quiet of the new year and celebrated my new sense of freedom.

12 What's Changed

From my early youth I knew there was something different about me. I daydreamed often (a testament of my third-grade teacher) of being a prince from some far-off land, certain one day my people would find me and everything would suddenly be intuitively obvious to the world. As I grew older and comprehended more of what society expected of me as a man, reality became intuitively obvious.

I was different from the social norm. While I eventually discovered others like me, they weren't going to come to my rescue. They were too preoccupied with hiding and trying to survive in a society that considered us repulsive. Instead of hiding, I found the courage to step out and be forward about my sexual orientation as an agent of change. I had to confront my fears in order to find the opportunities—certainly, the course of my career and life took a new direction. I would like to think the lives of others in the workplace have also improved.

A friend asked me how much has really changed for GLBT employees in the workplace over the past decade. So let's explore reality. According to *HRC State of the Workplace* reports, there has been some significant progress:

- While there is still no federal protection against discrimination on the basis of sexual orientation, 20 states and the District of Columbia have laws providing such protection in both the public and private sector (HRC, 2006-2007).

- Gender identity's another story—a little over ten years ago only Minnesota offered protection against job discrimination on the basis of gender identity in the public and private sector. Today there are 12 states and the District of Columbia (HRC, 2006-2007).

- Virtually a non-issue a decade ago, same-sex marriage and civil unions seem to be popping up on the legislative agendas of many states today. At the time of this writing 26 states have amended their constitutions to restrict marriage as between a man and a woman (HRC, 2008). Additionally, 19 other states have passed laws restricting marriage.

- The debate over same-sex marriage was ignited when Massachusetts became the first state to offer same-sex couples marriage licenses in 2004. Connecticut, New Jersey and Vermont offer civil unions, with several other states having legislated most of the state benefits of marriage to same sex couples (HRC, 2006-2007).

- Over 2,800 businesses include sexual orientation in their non-discrimination policies (HRC, 2004). Among the Fortune 500 companies, 88 percent have sexual orientation in their non-discrimination policies (HRC, 2005-2006).

- Even the issue of discrimination on the basis of gender identity/expression has made strides in recent years. Today there are more than 125 Fortune 500 businesses that include gender identity and/or expression in their non-discrimination polices. In 1999 only two Fortune 500 companies had such protections (HRC, 2006-2007).

- Domestic partner benefits, a rarity a decade ago, are now offered by more than 8,000 businesses (HRC State of the Workplace Report, 2004). Currently, more than half of the Fortune 500 companies (267) now offer the benefits (HRC, 2006-2007).

- Many companies have established GLBT employee network/affinity groups that are recognized by their employers, some even receiving company funding.
- Advertising dollars funneling into the GLBT media continue to rise as businesses try to tap into the growing GLBT market. The market research firm Packaged Facts estimates the buying power of the GLBT community to exceed $835 billion by 2011. According to the *2004 Gay Press Report* (Prime Access & Rivendell Media), advertising in gay media grew more than 28 percent in 2006, with more than 150 Fortune 500 brands tapping into the GLBT media market.
- Some businesses are even learning how to stave off the threats of conservative right-wing boycotts (albeit the hard way). Most recently, Ford Motors and Microsoft come to mind. Conservative groups took credit for Ford's discontinuing marketing of their high-end vehicles in the GLBT media and Microsoft's pulling support from a bill that would have prohibited discrimination on the basis of sexual orientation and gender identity in Washington State. After consultation with GLBT groups, both companies clarified their positions, with Microsoft reinstating support for the state bill and Ford planning to advertise a broader portfolio of their vehicles in the GLBT media.
- Even Shell made remarkable progress after 1994. The company has a vibrant and active GLBT employee network group in the U.S., with other chapters formed in the UK and the Netherlands. The company added sexual orientation to their non-discrimination policy in 1996 and began offering domestic partner benefits in 1998. Shell

> was even the first major energy company to endorse the Employment Non-Discrimination Act (ENDA) in 2002. Through involvement in GLBT community organizations, the company continues to leave a positive impression. The company also made a notable appearance in 2006 when they had a "float" in the Amsterdam Gay Pride parade—a barge parade on the canals. The crowning achievement occurred in 2008 with the inclusion of gender identity in the company nondiscrimination policy.

Progress toward creating a safe, open work environment where everyone has the opportunity to achieve his or her full potential has been remarkable. So why are there so few openly gay top executives in corporations? Why is it still okay for many employees and managers to make disparaging remarks about the GLBT community to their peers and superiors? Why aren't more companies supporting legislation that levels the playing field for GLBT employees in the workplace? Why are companies struggling with adding gender identity to their non-discrimination policies? Why does corporate support for the GLBT community waver when challenged by conservative right-wing organizations?

I think the answers to these questions are directly related to governance, education, and corporate culture. The following points flesh out some of my personal observations pertaining to the evolution of acceptance of GLBT employees in the workplace:

▶ **Some influential companies still aren't on board with inclusive workplace policies.** Some companies have done very well by concentrating on the letter of the law and pursuing strong fiscal governance. Take for example ExxonMobil. They have repeatedly shown strong financial earnings and set profit records for their industry segment, and for corporate America.

Yet ExxonMobil has refused to explicitly extend the protections of their non-discrimination policy beyond those categories covered by existing laws. In fact, after numerous years of proxy battles over adding sexual orientation to the ExxonMobil Equal Employment Opportunity policy, the company still refuses, even though shareholders controlling about a third of the stock support the change. To justify their position, the company has repeatedly said it does not discriminate. This stance seems well aligned with the culture and governing principles of the company.

▶ **While many companies have modified their policies, programs and systems to enable a more inclusive work environment for GLBT employees, putting these changes into practice seems to be more sporadic.** Basically, the words are on paper, but the practices are not consistently embedded throughout the organization. Some reasons for this:

- When it comes to embedding inclusive behaviors into the culture of a company, managers may feel poorly equipped (i.e. tools, resources or training), especially in tackling issues pertaining to sexual orientation/gender identity in the workplace.
- With ever-changing business pressures, the bottom line metrics often appear to dominate over workplace issues. The business focuses on products and deliverables instead of on productivity and who is making the deliverables.
- HR may not be completely up to the task either. They tend to focus on maintaining people systems that are cost effective, refining them periodically to remain competitive for talent. Sexual orientation and gender identity may seem like a microscopic issue requiring an exponential amount of time to manage effectively with little return. However, a growing number of companies are seeing some of these benefits and policies as effective recruiting tools for the younger generation coming into the workplace.

During a recent workshop on GLBT workplace issues, I illustrated to business leaders the cost of lost productivity associated with GLBT employees' not being out in the workplace. After I made my point, the HR representative countered by sharing that support of GLBT inclusion and company sponsorship of GLBT community events also carried a cost in the form of productivity loss—the work created for HR and management when employees exercise their right to voice objections based on their religious beliefs and personal values.

Missing from the HR perspective was a distinction between productivity loss from people hiding a portion of their identity and not feeling they're living up to a company's expected behaviors (e.g. trust, dignity, respect, honesty), and productivity loss associated with not modeling those expected behaviors by sending out e-mails critical of being inclusive. I believe companies should respect the values and beliefs of their employees. Equally important, employees should understand and respect the expected behaviors of a company when at work. To put this in perspective:

- I have yet to understand how e-mails and conversations in which disparaging remarks are made about GLBT employees or the community live up to these expected behaviors.

- It's difficult to create a safe, open work environment without addressing these issues on the same level as with other protected groups (e.g. race, religion, gender, veteran status, disabilities, etc.).

- Gay & lesbian employees have legislated protection from workplace discrimination in less than half of the states and a patchwork of municipalities. Without the passage of a national piece of legislation that offers protection from workplace discrimination on the bases of sexual orientation and gender identity, it becomes difficult for a GLBT employee to bring his or her whole "self" to work.

- For the transgender community the blanket of protection from workplace discrimination and provisions for health benefits might best be described as "threadbare." Those protections and benefits extended to gay, lesbian, and bisexual employees should also be available to transgender employees.

► **Changing corporate culture to become more inclusive starts at the top and must be maintained from the top.** Leaders are responsible for creating a vision for the company. They are stewards, shepherding the businesses toward achieving the vision, maintaining a hawkish eye on ethics, compliance, and fiscal and social responsibility. I think some characteristics of good leaders are that they:

- Lead the change process, taking prudent risks, stepping out of their comfort zone and broadening their learning.
- Realize their most valuable assets are the people keeping their capital investments operational and financially productive.
- Recognize the value of recruiting and retaining the best and the brightest talent, and promoting innovation and new ideas as part of a business case for embracing diversity and inclusion.

Yet when inclusion extends to embracing GLBT employees and their community, some leaders tend to "blink." By blink, I mean they tend to back down. There are a number of reasons for this observation:

- Some companies or divisions may deem themselves "not ready" to undertake training on GLBT workplace issues, shying away from these and other tough issues.
- Because the organization may be deemed "not ready," managers moving up through the talent pipeline and suc-

cession process may have no real grounding on GLBT issues.

- Sustaining a safe, inclusive culture requires an educational component, review and hardwiring of systems and processes, and a degree of accountability by everyone in adhering to the values and business principles of the company.

▶ **People tend to embrace those things they're most familiar or comfortable with, preferring the "known" to the "unknown."** The recent battle over changing the structure of the Social Security system to include private investment accounts is a good example. The changes were proposed to empower people with a say in how they invest their Social Security dollars for the future. The unknown was whether people would be any better or worse off from their private investment accounts. The uncertainty made many uncomfortable.

By nature, people don't step out en mass and embrace change. The process can be slow. As people understand what's changing and how it impacts them personally, they tend to be more comfortable in their decision process. The same is true about GLBT workplace issues. My experience has been that those people who take the time to understand the issues tend to be supportive.

▶ **What makes the unknown known—education, education, education.** Those leaders who develop a reasonable level of knowledge on workplace issues seem the most empowered to level the playing field for GLBT employees and others. Not including sexual orientation and gender identity training in the curriculum leaves managers and employees vulnerable when promoting a more inclusive work environment and policies for employees.

SEA Shell provided educational venues to employees on sexual orientation as a workplace issue—in 2004, about 1,000 people attended these sessions. Yet attendance was often voluntary. Ironically, some of those doing the training were working for managers who couldn't reconcile their personal beliefs with the company's desire to create a safe, open workplace inclusive of GLBT employees.

Hardwiring sexual orientation/gender identity training into the education systems of a company is one way of reaching more people. The Westhollow Technologies Center successfully hardwired sexual orientation into some of their diversity training for managers. When pursuing work on another tough workplace topic, inclusion of white males in diversity, workshops were designed with a component on sexual orientation as well as issues of racism, heterosexism, and power and privilege.

▶ **Changes in leadership may impede people from coming out.** GLBT employees struggle with coming out when company leadership seems to change every three or four years, with each new CEO bringing a fresh agenda. In this day and age of corporate mergers and acquisitions, shifting attitudes and cultures may impact whether diversity and inclusion emerges as a business imperative. The changing governance structures may encourage businesses to make decisions about diversity that could be interpreted as a signal the company is not as inclusive as suggested.

▶ **Walk the talk—think about what you can do to demonstrate support for GLBT employees.** People who tend to be the strongest advocates for GLBT employees are those who have taken the time to understand the topic as it relates to the workplace. There are many resources (books, websites, community organizations, employee affinity groups, etc.) available to help people understand what the issues are in the workplace and how heterosexual allies can be more supportive and inclusive.

I think of Judy and Steve as two examples of people who made time to learn about GLBT workplace issues. There are a number of ways GLBT employees can help with the learning process:

- Partner with leaders to understand where they are on GLBT workplace issues and explore some of the barriers preventing them from being more supportive.
- Conduct or participate in workshops with managers and leaders in which sexual orientation/gender identity comprises some or all of the learning. Hearing from people in their own organization can send a powerful message to managers and colleagues.
- I've found that forwarding key articles or references can be helpful for continued learning. Remember, time is a valuable commodity in the workplace, so try to be strategic and objective in what you choose to send.
- Bring up current events like gay marriage, adding gender identity to non-discrimination policies, adoption issues for GLBT couples, immigration issues, etc. with managers to support their learning.
- Develop talking points on key issues, the business case for being inclusive, and pending legislation that might affect GLBT employees in the company (ENDA, domestic partner benefits, tax issues, immigration issues for domestic partners, etc.). Talking points are a convenient method of articulating the key messages consistently to various audiences.
- Explore speaking opportunities for company leaders and others at key conferences. These can be effective venues for sharing progress, enhancing reputation in the community, and broadening learning through identifying the best practices from other companies.
- Critique and coach those wanting to sharpen their effectiveness in addressing GLBT workplace issues. People make mistakes—that's part of life. Helping leaders know

what they got right and where there's room for improvement in a safe learning environment can sharpen their effectiveness in creating an inclusive workplace.

There is room at the table for sexual orientation and gender identity to be worked on along with other facets of diversity. These two topics and others, such as disabilities, age, power and privilege, micro-inequities, culture, etc. tend to transcend race and gender.

► **Even diversity departments can shy away from tough issues.** The work around race and gender is not easy. I've worked in the field of diversity for many years. I've rolled up my sleeves on creating equitable systems for recruiting, retention, development and advancement of women and people of color in the workplace. But a more diverse leadership doesn't automatically equate to creating a more inclusive workplace.

Everyone has some learning to do around tough topics in the workplace. Even diversity departments have a continuing role in self-education and awareness to understand the impacts on the workplace of ever-evolving issues and topics in the workplace. I often reflect on my own personal learning and that of my colleagues from Sara on the issues pertaining to gender identity and what it was like for me as a diversity professional to become comfortable with the topic. At times I'm sure she felt completely alone.

► **If you're not part of the solution, you're part of the problem.** This was something Nelson, my colleague who left Shell and catalyzed my coming out process, would tell me early on in my journey.

- Ultimately everyone has a hand in creating the workplace and making it safe.
- Whether someone is out, in the closet, or a straight ally, there are things each person can do to promote fairness.

- If you're waiting for leaders to do the work by themselves, you may be waiting a very long time. Check in to see how they're doing and offer to partner in identifying areas where they may require help.

A few years ago a colleague shared that he and others had met with the leaders of Shell in Europe as part of an awareness session on GLBT workplace issues. By the end of their meeting the leaders had agreed to work several action items and get back with the employees on their progress. The leaders missed a deadline, and my colleague viewed this as an indication of lack of interest. When asked what he and others had done to support the leaders, I had a sense the expectation was for the leaders to do all the work.

- It's important to assess the ability of leaders (knowledge, resources, time given to other commitments, etc.) to adequately follow up on actions.
- I personally don't believe in having a meeting with leaders, developing actions and hoping I won't be disappointed. I tend to make it a personal commitment to help them be successful in achieving their actions.
- Knowing the stakes and having a sense of other pressures facing leaders, look for opportunities to reconnect on how things are shaping up and offer assistance.
- Assisting leaders in their learning journey can build avenues for stronger relationships and trust.
- Leaders still have to do the learning and decide appropriate actions for themselves and their organizations. You can't do the work for them—just help leaders be more efficient in their learning by identifying key resources or opportunities supporting their development.

Looking back, the one thing remaining consistent is the inconsistency of the level of tolerance in the work environment for people wanting to come out. People are in different places when it comes to change depending on how they weigh the potential risks and opportunities to themselves. Coming out is a journey—some parts of the company are going to be supportive and inclusive, and others are not. In creating a level of consistency, I think companies need to consider the right balance of expectations for personal commitment and compliance.

I have learned from GLBT and heterosexual role models in my life that there's no manual that comes with leadership. I don't believe someone can be trained to be a leader; I do believe training can "awaken" some of those skills and competencies he or she already possesses. Some of these competencies are:

- Humility—I don't have all the right answers, and at times I may be wrong, but I accept responsibility for my actions.
- Valuing and Involving Others—People bring different views and perspectives to the table. I believe leveraging these differences enhances innovation and creativity. One of my key lessons from Steve as CEO was that having a broad foundation of opinions helped to formalize more effective decisions.
- Empathic Listening—I had to learn to meet people where they were on a variety of topics and then decide how or if to move forward from there. I learned to listen to what life was like for others rather than making my own assumptions.
- Patience and Persistence—Change in large corporations can evolve at a glacial pace. Patience and persistence are important attributes for staying the course. Shell didn't endorse ENDA on the first try. Gender identity wasn't added to the Shell non-discrimination policy on the first

try. I believe through persistence and patience, they'll get there one day.

- Integrity—I've received hate mail, had conversations with people comparing me to pedophiles and alcoholics, and heard managers speak against a work environment inclusive of GLBT employees. Throughout these episodes I've deliberately maintained a sense of integrity, not wanting to stoop to their tactics.

- Strength—Throughout my career, situations arose when I just wanted to quit because I didn't think I had the strength or stamina. Strength comes from many sources. I get my strength from Slava, my mentors, and close friends. They were the people who helped me find the energy.

- Courage—Like most people, I struggle with facing my fears. Yet doing so is what courage is all about. Coming out in the workplace was something I feared, but I learned to overcome the anxiety by understanding the "beasts" that kept me awake at night.

Among my role models were Judy, Richard, Sara, Steve, and friends from other companies with whom I served on the HRC Business Council. They all instilled the importance of being a strong role model; maintaining a balance between my zeal for GLBT workplace issues and credibility with leaders; understanding that "no" doesn't necessarily mean "no"; courage coming from within; and most importantly, having a clear vision of where I was going.

The decisions I made were based on one simple vision: creating a safe, open workplace where everyone is treated with dignity and respect and has the ability to achieve his or her full potential. My metrics for progress have to be tangible—if I can't see the results in the workplace, then neither can a closeted individual struggling with coming out. Knowing a leader is supportive isn't enough; he or she has to be engaged in creating change. Some examples of tangibility could be a department manager requiring sexual orientation/gender identity education for all managers and employees in the organization, supporting the company GLBT employee group in achieving their goals, not tolerating derogatory jokes about GLBT people, or modeling expected behaviors for inclusiveness.

There were some great moments along the road—adding sexual orientation to Shell's non-discrimination policy, meeting Judy and Richard, creating SEA Shell, watching some of the first couples sign up for domestic partner benefits, presiding over the commitment ceremony of Vickie and Clyde, the HRC Business Council, Shell's endorsement of ENDA, and the privilege of working with Steve while he was CEO.

There were also hardships, such as my first hate mail, an e-mail from an employee disgusted with the addition of sexual orientation to the company non-discrimination policy. I learned to move beyond the hurt, searching for the bigger picture and making rational decisions for the good of the whole.

The most devastating blow was the loss of my beloved mentor and friend, Richard. A huge void was left by his departure—with his passing I realized that at some point you have to walk alone to find your place in life. While he is no longer a physical presence in my life, I still have the memories and the lessons we shared in my growth and development.

Life since coming out almost fourteen years ago hasn't been easy, and from the very beginning no one ever said it would be. If offered the option to do it all again, I would, simply because I'd like to think my efforts made the lives of others a little better, and companies a little wiser. As for the future—there's still the path ahead.